An Instruction Manual for Food Dreams by

D. ERIC PETTIGREW

ISBN: 9781916889088

headfire publishing limited
london

www.headfire.co.uk

Follow on Instagram @whitetigerfooddreams

If you have the interactive version, click on the title below on each page to return to the Table of Contents or the Icon to go to the Index

Around the world in 80 recipes
WHITETIGER
FOOD DREAMS

All good food starts with a dream.

Ah...but to turn that dream into an actual dish.

You must start with the ingredients. Not just the main components of the dish, but its provenance, quality and freshness.

You make a plan in your head, and continue on with a method, which involves preparation, and time.

You select the right tools for the job.

You arrange everything in advance.

And then you start the clock, which begins a process which for a myriad of reasons is different every time.

There is no such thing as a recipe for success. A recipe is only a suggestion.

The rest is experiment, learning from failure, concentration and that special moment of inspiration that comes when you are in mid-stream.

For my beloved wife Steens
and my son Roman

Who have both endured my obsession with food
whether or not they ate the dishes I dreamed of.

食べ物夢

たべものゆめ

FOOD DREAMS

Food is the lifeforce
Which nourishes your body
Food dreams feed the soul.

SPAGHETTI FALSI DI CETRIOLI
SMOKED HADDOCK
CHOWDER
BONE MARROW
CHEESEBURGER
JACK HAWKINS BUN
LOVE PIE
POMODORI
SEA BREAM
WITH LENTILS
ZUPPA DI COZZE
PUMPKIN PIE
RISOTTO NERO FRUTTI DI MARE

料理と暮らし

りょうりとくらし

COOKING AND LIVING

Your philosophy
Of cooking should be the same
As that of living.

Rudyard Kipling once said:

I have six strong serving men / They taught me all I know / Their names are Who and What and When and Why and Where and How.

Before you even start to read this book, you have to ask yourself some questions: Am I a dreamer or not? Am I an adventurer who would rather fail at something new that do the same thing over and over again? Do I ever dream of food?

If the honest answers to these questions is No, you probably haven't even got this far.

*But if the answer is Yes, then this book may help you. Why? Because cooking is one of the few things in life you can do **every** day where the only critic you have is yourself, and where you can try whatever dreams you may have with little adverse consequences. Fail? Pitch it in the bin, remember the lesson, and try another day. Those are the potential negative results, but they are far outweighed by the positive ones.*

This book assumes you know nothing about cooking. Nothing.

It gives you a map to follow, starting with the ***tools*** *you will need, an explanation of the* ***heat sources****, what should be in your* ***storehouse****, the* ***ingredients*** *you can choose from, the* ***skills*** *you will use, the* ***science*** *behind cooking, the different* ***cooking methods****, and ah yes...****recipes.***

This is not a recipe book, although there are 80 different recipes from a variety of cuisines, allowing you to take an Around-the-World-in-Eighty-Days tour of global food.

This book is a road map to your imagination.

This book will answer the questions What, When, Where and How? It is up to you to answer Who and Why?

This is an instruction manual for you to create your own food dreams.

Good luck on your journey.

ERIC

Kew, ENGLAND

December, 2023

Why WHITETIGER?

When I lived in Korea working for Chase Manhattan Bank, one of my former students looked at the Chinese character name given to me in Hong Kong, shook his head and said: 'Not good.' I asked him what it meant. He said: 'Well-taken care of by the Emperor,' scowling dismissively.

He said that parents asked him to name their children, and that he would come back to me the next day with a proper name. The next morning he threw a card on my desk. It said: **白大虎** *. White Great Tiger. Beck Dae Ho in Korean (which sounded a bit like Pettigrew). 'Your new name', he said. Thank you, Kim Soo In.*

Changed my life. Names are everything. The chop I had made is a legal signature.

What's with the KANJI AND HAIKU?

I started writing haiku in the middle of the night (a-later-in-life development) to quieten my mind. I find the discipline of having to say something in 17 syllables liberating. It is much the same as a recipe for food. Constraint within boundaries coupled with imagination means freedom.

So writing haiku for the subjects in the book seemed logical.

But just like food, the immense variations and complexity of the Japanese language (in particular) will never be mastered. Kanji is like the saying: The known is a drop. The unknown an ocean.

Thanks to Tet Ogino, the most egregious errors have been caught, but just as with recipes and food, there is no one correct way of saying things in every language. It depends.

NAVIGATION

*INTERACTIVE VERSION: The hardest part about finding your way around a complex subject is knowing where to look. Navigation around either the printed or interactive version of this book is either the **table of contents**, or by the **index**, or by specific **cross-references. See below how to get the Interactive version.***

These are easily reached by clicking at the bottom of the page the Table of Contents of Index, or on a specific link as shown below.

WHITETIGER FOOD DREAMS

Clicking on the badge takes you to the INDEX

Clicking on the TITLE takes you to the Table of Contents

(See COOKING RICE on page 74)

Clicking on an orange link will take you to the relevant page for the topic

GET THE INTERACTIVE PDF VERSION

Scan this QR code with your phone or iPad. You will have to provide your email address and full name and confirm you have purchased the book or been given it as a gift.

Then you can download the InteractivePDF.

TABLE OF CONTENTS

INTERACTIVE VERSION: Click on icon or text or page number

WHITETIGER FOOD DREAMS

WHITETIGER FOOD DREAMS

TOOLS

がかのどうぐ

ARTIST'S TOOLS

Artists are only
As good as the tools they use
To create their art.

COOKING TOOLS

You wouldn't think of playing tennis without a proper racquet. Why would you cook without the right tool?

Cooking can be broken down into peeling, chopping, mixing, grating, mashing, drizzling, marinating, and a myriad of other tasks before you actually start producing or cooking something. Then there is the question of what receptacle to use to cook the dish, how to serve and how to store it.

The most important tool is your knife. Buy the highest quality and keep it sharp, using a whetstone. Old school.

The second most important tool is a good mixer/spice grinder. The Cuisinart stainless steel one is perfect for the full range of uses. Spices, smoothies, mayonnaise, coulis. You name it.

The third most important is a spoon/spatula. I am partial to silicon, different colours for savoury and sweet.

Think long and hard about the tools you buy. Never scrimp, but go for simplicity.

It should be very clear when you reach for something what job it is for and how versatile it can be.

Use your wits to improvise. The best solution is sometimes the simplest.

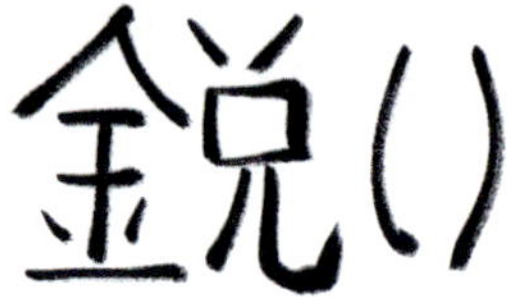

するどい

SHARP

When in the kitchen
Keep your knives sharpened
And your wits sharper.

TOOLS

COOKING TOOLS

CUTTING TOOLS (GLOBAL KNIVES)

Paring 10cm | Utility 13cm | Chopper 18cm | Chef's 20cm | Chinese Chopper | Breadknife | Pastry Knife | Poultry Shears | Scissors | Can Opener

MANUAL TOOLS

Silicone Spatulas | Tongs | Peelers/Julienne | Whisk | Frother | Cheese Grater | Cheese Slicer | Zester | Basting Brushes | Apple Corer | Avocado Scooper

Wok Utensils | Ladle | Wok Strainer | Metal Spatula | Pounder | Potato Masher | Pestle & Mortar | Sifter | Strainer | Colander | Opener/Corkscrew

GIZMOS

Spice Grinder | Blender | Handheld | Food Processor | Hand Mixer | Spiralizer | Mandolin

SALAD

Oil Drizzler | Salad Shaker | Salad Spinner | Salad Bowl

COOKING CONTAINERS

Pots and Pans | Steamer | Frying Pan | Wok | Casserole | Griddle Pan | Omelette Pan

Ceramic Casseroles, Gratinee, & Pie Dish | Copper Minis | Roasting Tins | Pizza Pan | Egg Poachers

RECEPTACLES

Jar with Lid | Plastic Storage | Glass Bowls | Ramikins

Storage Jar | Measuring Cup & Spoons | Cake rings

TOP 12 TOOLS

Looking at the myriad of tools available, it might seem intimidating, or expensive, or both. Here is a list of the top 12 that I use. I have left out some (like a whisk, for instance). The most used implement in my kitchen is the Cuisinart spice grinder, which I use for everything. Smoothies. Sauces. Salad dressings. Dry spices. You name it. And the top? The knife, of course. It goes without saying. The most time-saving is the olive oil drizzler. And the most practical? The simple silicone spoon.

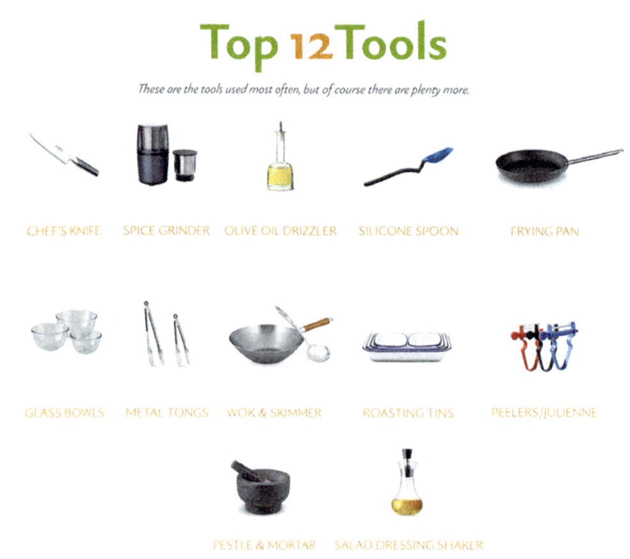

ORGANISING YOUR TOOLS

We all have limited workspace, and accumulate gizmos and gadgets over the years. Ralph Waldo Emerson once wrote: Simplify. Simplify. Simplify. He might have been talking about the kitchen.

However, it is easier said than done. Each task may have its appropriate tool which you feel you cannot do without. So be it.

Organise them by groups. By function. By height. By frequency of use. Use drawer utensil inserts with expandable dividers. Use containers specifically for the longer utensils on the counter. Give it some thought.

To alter Emerson's words slightly: Organise. Organise. Organise.

It will save you no end of hassle.

Limited space requires organisation.

HEAT SOURCES

ねっき

HEAT

Heat comes from the sun
Usually, that is, but
Not in the kitchen.

HEAT SOURCES

When you cook, not only are you playing with fire, you are playing with heat.

And heat comes in many different guises.

Conduction. Convection. Radiation. Steaming. Boiling. Dry. Gentle. Harsh. Gas. Electric. Downward. Upward.

Heat is not just a question of temperature of the source.

It is also a function of the weight and size, texture, thickness, water content, and sensitivity of what is being cooked

Flavours blend at low heat, with different results if liquid or dry. Sugars caramelise at a high heat, but not too hot or else they carbonise.

It is practically impossible to brown a wet object, whether it be a piece of meat or vegetable.

Some foods benefit from rapid heat changes.

Batter crisps if made with ice cold carbonated water. High heat on a hob is not the same as high heat in the oven. There is truth to the saying: if you can't stand the heat, get out of the kitchen.

Learn to respect and embrace heat, or flounder like a fish in the sand.

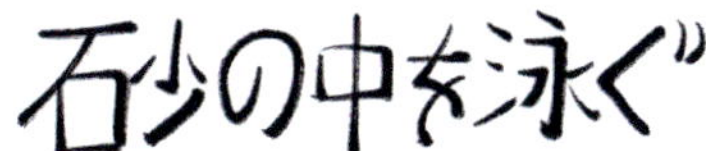

すなのなかをおよぐ

SWIMMING IN SAND

Not understanding
Heat when you are cooking is
Like swimming in sand.

TEMPERATURE CONVERSION

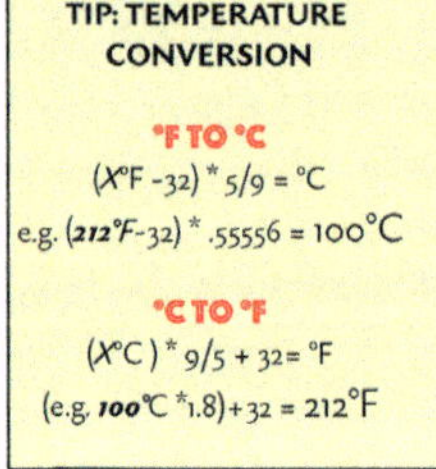

TEMPERATURE CONVERSION CHART

Gas Mark	°F	°C	Fan °C
1	275	140	120
2	300	150	130
3	325	170	150
4	350	180	160
5	375	190	170
6	400	200	180
7	425	220	200
8	450	230	210
9	475	240	220

STOREHOUSE

ゆめのおきば

The storehouse of dreams

The inner sanctum
Of kitchens is the cupboard
The storehouse of dreams.

SPICE TYPES

We tend to think of spices as being wedded to a certain type of cuisine- Indian is the most obvious. Or Thai. Or Szechuan. Or Italian. The reality is that spices are very versatile.

They also change. Dry spices become wet. Spices release their flavour by being roasted or ground, by being blended into sauces, or sautéed with onions or garlic, or rubbed into meat.

A spice should never overwhelm, but should turn up unexpectedly in the corners of the mouth or in the mind, a subtle reminder of a sensation.

Just as important as the choice of spice is how you store them, how you blend them, and how to apply them.

Some spices are complementary. Some should be kept apart.

The only way to know is to introduce them to each other. Consider them as first dates, which may or may not work out.

Spices make life worth living.

They are the enemy of the bland, and the friend of the adventurous.

こうしんりょう

SPICE

A spice plants a seed
On the tongue that can flower
In the memory.

SPICES

MAIN

Sea salt | Black pepper | Celery Salt | Chili Flakes | Garlic | Ginger | Coriander Leaf | Cumin | Rosemary | Parsley

MEDITERRANEAN (FRENCH, ITALIAN, SPANISH)

Sage | Thyme | Tarragon | Bay Leaves | Truffle | Oregano | Basil | Peperoncino | Smoked Paprika | Saffron

Fennel | Mint | Chives | Dill | Fines Herbes | Nutmeg | Sesame | Cinnamon | Capers | Anchovies

ASIAN (CHINESE, THAI, JAPANESE)

5 Spice | Szechuan Pepper | Star Anise | Lemon Grass | Galangal | Fish Sauce | Kaffir Lime | Ponzu | Togarashi | Shiso

INDIAN

Coriander | Cardamom | Fenugreek | Turmeric | Mustard | Garam Masala | Cayenne | Curry Leaves | Cloves | Poppy Seeds

MIDDLE EASTERN & NORTH AFRICAN

Ras Al Hanout | Za'atar | Allspice | Sumac

FISH

Old Bay | Mace | Mustard Powder

BBQ

Brown Sugar | Hot Sauce | Lime Zest

SAUCES & CONDIMENTS

The sauciest things are the most interesting in life.

No one is moved by the insipid.

Some of the most sensitive organs in the body are the taste buds of the tongue, able to differentiate instantaneously tastes from a vast database of shared memories and real-time data, sometimes from the most minuscule of samples.

These amazing organs can immediately say whether something is too salty, icky-sweet, eye-watering spicy, bitter or sour.

They can remember not only the initial sensation, but the after-taste... echoes of stimulation. The umami of life.

Condiments can be added before, during, or after cooking. They can cure and age gracefully, or wake up a dish with a loud fanfare.

Sauces mellow from age and from blending, but like all the instruments of an orchestra they excel if no one taste drowns out the others.

Balance and variety are the key, just like the saying goes.

The spice of life.

みらい

Taste buds

Taste buds are tickled
Just as much by a salt flake
As by the whole bite.

SAUCES & CONDIMENTS

SEASONING

Sea salt | Smoked Salt | Celery Salt | Salt and Seaweed

PEPPER

Black Pepper | White Pepper | Szechuan Pepper | Chilli Flakes | Togarashi

UMAMI

Miso | Light Soy | Dark Soy | Tamari | Fish Sauce | Worcestershire | Dashi | Anchovies | Marmite | Doenjang | Shrimp Paste | Dried Mushrooms

SWEET

Honey | Brown Sugar | Palm Sugar | Date Syrup | Molasses | Caramel | Chocolate | Tahini | Maple Syrup | Teriyaki | Hoisin | Mirin | Sake

ACID (VINEGARS AND CITRUS)

Red | White | Cider | Sherry | Rice | Malt | Balsamic | Black | Ponzu | Yuzu | Lime | Lemon | Orange | Grapefruit

HOT SPICY

Peperoncino | Sriracha | Tabasco | Jalapeño | Harissa | Frank's | Dijon | English Mustard | Wasabi | Horseradish | Ginger | Gochujang | Yuzu Kosho

OILS & CONDIMENTS

Olive | Vegetable | Sesame | Sunflower | Coconut | Mayonnaise | Ketchup | Brown Sauce | Barbeque | Taramasalata | Peanut Butter

SPICE STORAGE

The sock rule. Stored neatly, socks are easy to retrieve. Chucked into an unruly heap in a drawer, just finding ones that match can take an eternity. Especially in the dark.

The same holds true for storing spices and condiments.

Take the time to store them in a logical manner. For instance, vinegars to the right, umami to the middle and the least used to the left. They will congregate there anyway.

Store spice jars on their sides when possible, with the print facing outwards. Saves digging.

Label stand-up jars.

Keep sea salt in a container you can put your hand into easily. I cannot remember the last time, if ever, I measured out a tablespoon of salt. With Maldon Sea flakes, it is either a pinch, two or three finger scoops, or a fistful.

Use a pepper grinder with fresh peppercorns. Never use pre-mixed pepper.

Keep an eye on the jar levels and buy in bulk, but not too much for the time frame. Like life, spices degrade over time.

Store many spices in your garden (i.e. at the very least rosemary, thyme, oregano, and a bay tree).Mother Nature will do your provisioning for you.

When possible, always buy the whole seeds and roast and grind them fresh. (This is a two minute job with the Cusinart spice grinder.)

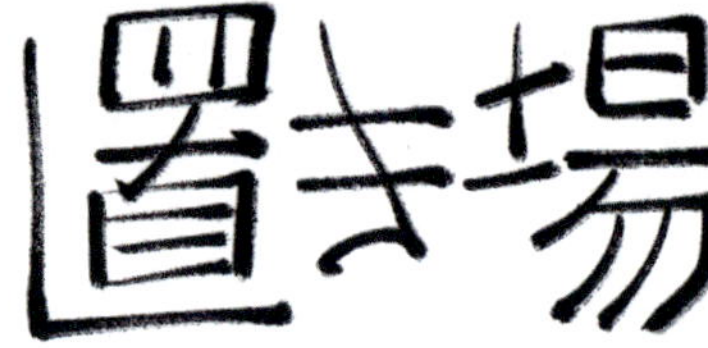

おきば

STOREHOUSE

Often the best place
To do your shopping will be
In your own cupboard.

BART
CELERY SALT
WHITE ROASTED SESAME SEEDS
CRUSHED CHILLIES
SAFFRON
by Sainsbury's

SOUS CHEF

PREMIUM
PONTI
AROMA ANTICO
MIRIN

Colman's Mustard

WHITETIGER
FOOD DREAMS

INGREDIENTS

ざいりょう

INGREDIENTS

Each ingredient
Is a colour with which to
Paint your own tableau.

BEEF

In cooking, red meat gets a raw deal. Not literally of course. For such an important source of protein, though, it gets pilloried.

But beef is omnipresent. Currently, 78% of the world population is NOT vegetarian, though as the world population grows this will drop.

It is good to know where the types of beef you eat come from on the animal. The cuts you eat may be a function of budget, taste and time. Don't scrimp on beef. Go for the highest quality if possible.

Roughly, the lower on the animal, the cheaper the cut, the tougher the meat, and the longer and slower and lower temperature the cooking.

Here is a brief guide.

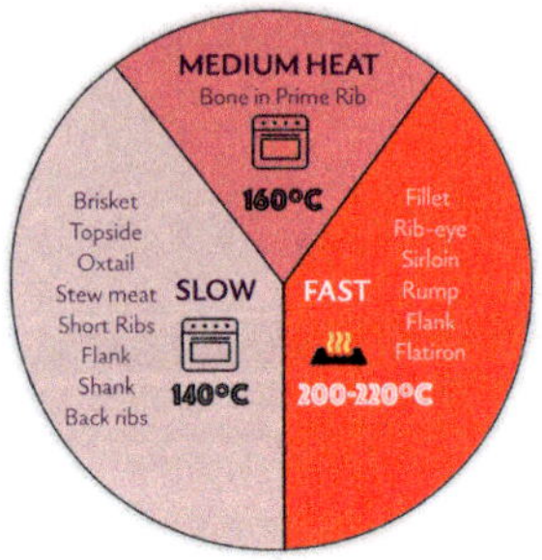

チャックワゴン

チャックワゴン

CHUCKWAGON

When the chuckwagon
Rolls up the cowpokes know
Topside from T-Bone.

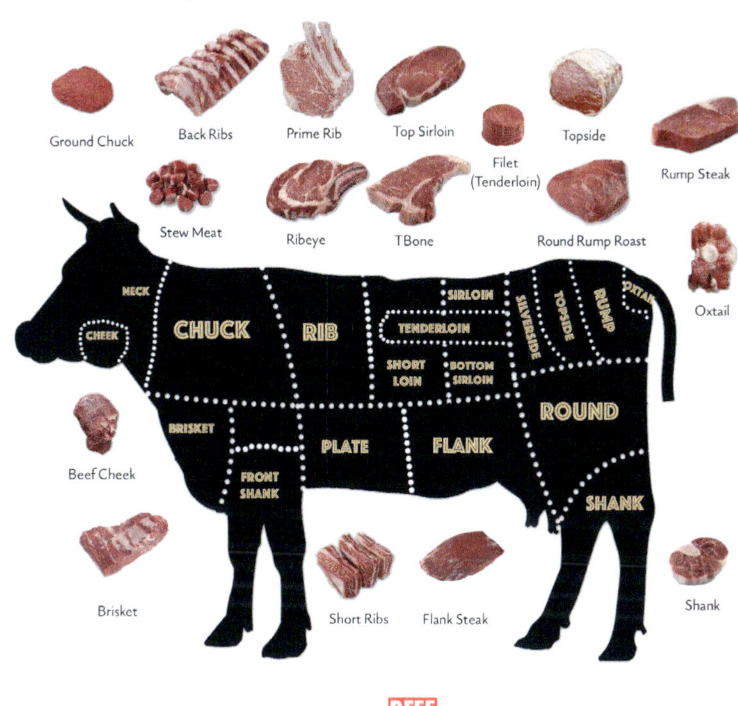

Ground Chuck
Back Ribs
Prime Rib
Top Sirloin
Filet
(Tenderloin)
Topside
Rump Steak
Stew Meat
Ribeye
TBone
Round Rump Roast
Oxtail
NECK
CHEEK
CHUCK
RIB
SIRLOIN
TENDERLOIN
SHORT
LOIN
BOTTOM
SIRLOIN
SILVERSIDE
TOPSIDE
RUMP
OXTAIL
BRISKET
PLATE
FLANK
ROUND
FRONT
SHANK
SHANK
Beef Cheek
Brisket
Short Ribs
Flank Steak
Shank

BEEF
CUTS

PORK

Pigs are never in a hurry.

The same can be said about their meat, with the exception of Bacon and Pancetta, both extremely high in fat content.

For many historical reasons, not the least of which is the possibility of illness from raw meat, pork wants to either be cured and smoked (to kill off bacteria). Nowadays, high quality pork raised correctly can be eaten slightly pink, but it also is a perfect foil for long slow cooking..

Because there is a lot of fat which likes to be rendered, often times you want to cook pork at a combination of high and low temperature.
The rule of thumb is Meat Slow and Low, Fat High and Dry.

Pork as a meat is extremely versatile, used throughout the day for breakfast, lunch and dinner. Every part of the animal gets used. Piggies don't die in vain.

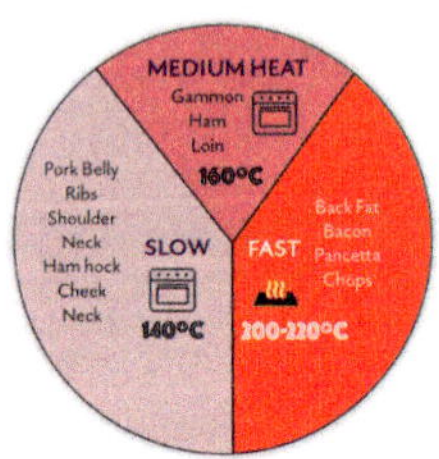

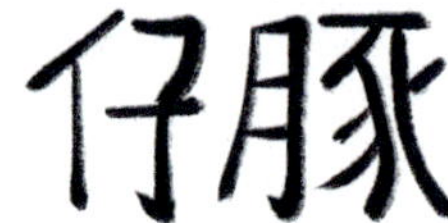

こぶた

LITTLE PIGGY

This little piggy
Went to market then fed us
All for a whole week.

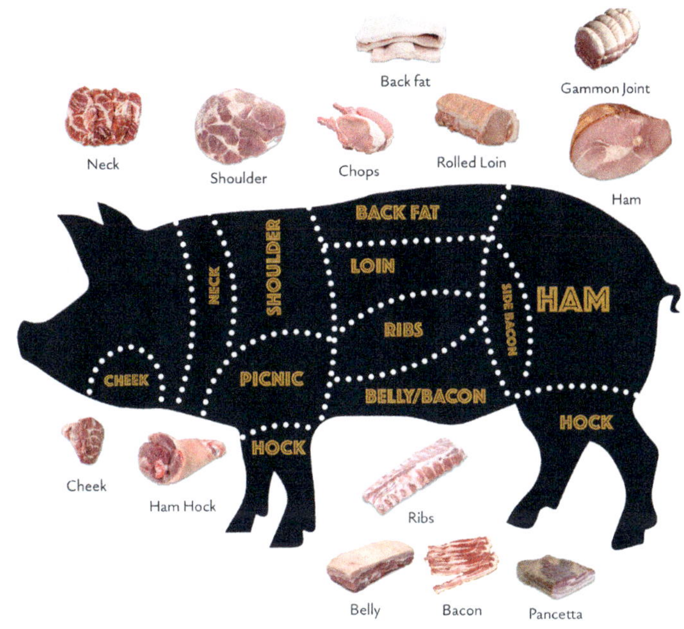

Back fat
Gammon Joint
Neck
Shoulder
Chops
Rolled Loin
Ham
BACK FAT
NECK
SHOULDER
LOIN
SIDE BACON
HAM
RIBS
CHEEK
PICNIC
BELLY/BACON
HOCK
HOCK
Cheek
Ham Hock
Ribs
Belly
Bacon
Pancetta

PORK
CUTS

LAMB

The silence of the lambs.

Anything but.

Lamb is a very strong meat whose taste is certainly not silent.

For the most part, the cuts of lambs are not tender and require careful care and attention.

Unlike pork, lamb can be eaten pink, but you strike a fine balance between tender pink and chewy red.

Certain cuts, like shoulder, shank, or leg, benefit from slow cooking.

Others, like flank steak, are not really steaks at all but should be cut cross-grain and used in dishes like stir-fried cumin lamb, after having been marinated and thus tenderised.

Ditto dishes using the cheeks, neck, and breast. Long and slow.

Lamb is inherently fatty, and thus the fat must be rendered at high heat. Many a lamb chop or rack of lamb has been ruined by not having the fat sufficiently rendered, or if rendered, the meat cooked into oblivion.

Lambs are small animals, but if you are thinking babies, think again. Having seen a few slaughtered in Argentina (indeed helping to slaughter one) you should consider them more of a sullen teenager rather than a cute toddler.

And yes, they are silent. Almost oblivious to their fate, which may be to provide nourishment and pleasure in a good meal.

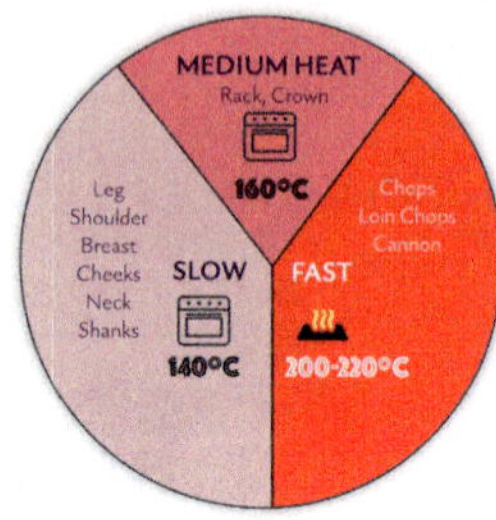

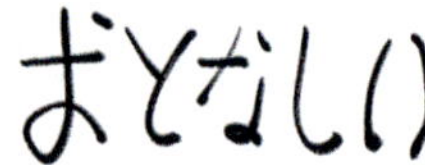

おとなしい

MEEK

The meek inherit
Or so the saying goes, but
No one told the lamb.

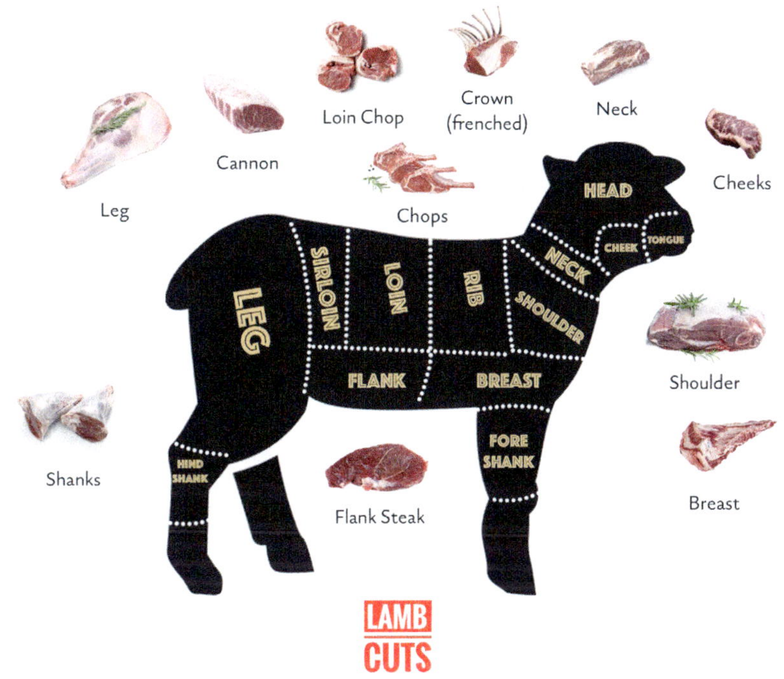

Loin Chop
Crown
(frenched)
Neck
Cannon
Cheeks
Leg
Chops
HEAD
CHEEK
TONGUE
NECK
LEG
SIRLOIN
LOIN
RIB
SHOULDER
Shoulder
FLANK
BREAST
Shanks
FORE
SHANK
HIND
SHANK
Flank Steak
Breast
LAMB
CUTS

POULTRY

Chicken is often regarded as poor man's steak. Ah, the humble chicken.

But it is safe to say there is no animal whose humble beginnings have created such a vast array of dishes, both regal and pedestrian.

Though cousins, a Brest Supreme de Volaille and a KFC chicken breast have no more in common than king and commoner .

And lest you think that a free range chicken or a plump chicken from the butcher and the three pound packet at the supermarket are the same thing, think again. That extra pound or two is eminently worth it.

Chicken can also be cooked in a bewildering number of ways. Grilled. Boiled. Roasted. Fried. Minced. Steamed. Baked.

It can be a curry, a salad, a soup, a sandwich, a Sunday lunch, a snack, a starter or main. It can be moussed or confited.

Every last bit can be used--the livers, the neck, the carcass.

Chicken stock is the **sine qua non** *of many dishes. Chicken soup may even have medicinal purposes, if grandmothers are to be believed.*

A young chicken...a poussin, can be as fine a meal as a filet mignon, and can be cooked in a jiff (well...23 minutes, to be precise).

Poor man's steak indeed.

As for the chicken's cousins-fowl- they are eaten less often but are no less versatile or tasty. The smaller the bird, like squab or quail, the harder to cook. The same with the large turkey. Both can dry out in a hurry.

ひよこちゃん

CHICKEN LITTLE

Chicken Little cried:
'The sky is falling!'; she must
Have been a free-range.

POULTRY

POULTRY & FOWL

CHICKEN

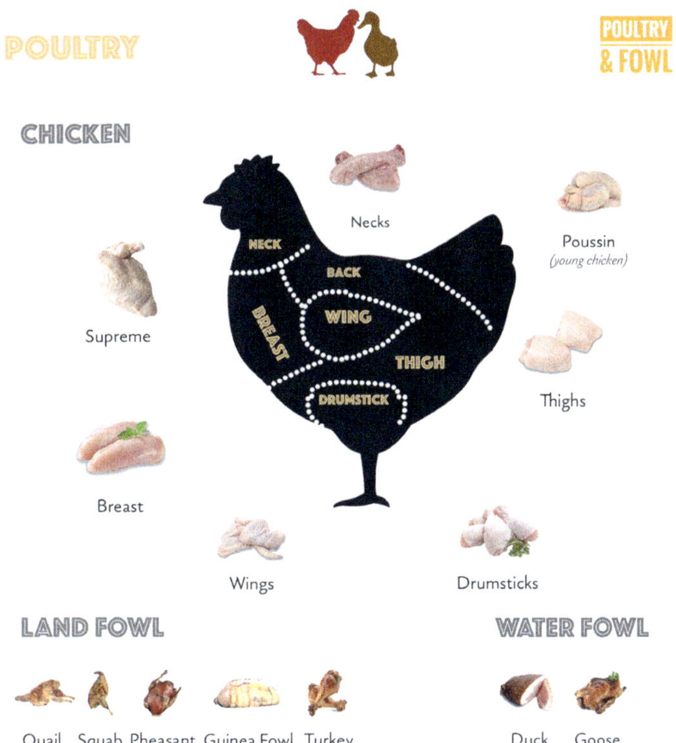

LAND FOWL

Quail Squab Pheasant Guinea Fowl Turkey

WATER FOWL

Duck Goose

SEAFOOD

If you were to eat every major type of seafood every day, you could go a month without ever eating the same dish.

And that is every MAJOR type, from fish to shellfish to crustaceans to molluscs.

Seafood is the greatest source of protein on the planet, yet if you asked me how much of it I ate, I would be off by a country mile.

We eat fish a lot, but seldom as a main course. In a restaurant, I would rarely order it over some other protein.

But I eat it all the time. In pasta. Raw. Or use it as seasoning (anchovies play a prominent role in so many dishes.)

Seafood sits comfortably as a starter, so unobtrusive and common as to be invisible (think smoked salmon).

Scallops on squid ink risotto elevate a tiny shellfish up to superstar status.

Lobster is the king of shellfish, and there is hardly a richer dish on the planet than a lobster bisque made up of the shells.
A simple fillet of sole can be the maestro of the restaurant orchestra.

But face it, who wants or knows how to gut, scale, or fillet a fish? Or peel the shell of a prawn and suck the juices out of the head? Or cook the octopus tentacle until it is soft? Or clean a crab and separate the brown and white meat

Just ask anyone who has ever lived near the sea though. It is worth it.

さめのかんがえ

Shark Thoughts

When a shark sees fish
Does he think to himself: Oh,
Look! There's some seafood!

SEAFOOD
OILY FISH
Salmon
Tuna
Trout
Mackerel
Anchovies
FISH
WHITE FISH
Cod
Haddock
Halibut
Hake
Bream
Flounder
Red Snapper
Sole
SMOKED/PICKLED
Kippers
Smoked Mackerel
Salmon/Gravalax
Herring
SEAFOOD TYPES
SASHIMI
Tuna (Maguro)
Salmon (Sake)
Yellowtail
ROE
Taramasalata
Salmon Roe/Caviar
SHELLFISH
CRUSTACEAN
MOLLUSKS
Oysters
Clams
Mussels
Scallops
Prawns
Shrimp
Lobster
Crab
Crayfish
Squid
Octopus

PASTA & GRAINS

There is no crop which has played a greater role in world civilisation then the different types of rice and grains which are consumed across the planet.

None more so than in Italy and in Asia, where pasta and rice are the staple of every diet.

But far from daily gruel, the varieties and permutations of both grain and pasta are immense.

Take pasta. There are at least 26 different varieties of Italian pasta, depending on whether or not they are ribbon-cut, tiny morsels, tube-shaped, or stuffed.

The quality varies widely, as do the cooking times. Durum wheat pasta takes longer to cook (10-12 minutes). Fresh pasta can take only 1-2 minutes.

Rice is a staple in Asia, but there is a large difference between the basmati rice of South Asia, sticky rice in Thailand., and sushi rice in Japan. Not to mention risotto rice in Italy (Arborio) or paella rice (Valencia) in Spain.

The consistency can vary enormously as well. Rice can be chewy, creamy, or fluffy. Fried rice is a way of recycling as well

Other grains also deserve mention. The cous cous of North Africa. Polenta. Hominy grits in the US. Barley (grown everywhere) or quinoa from South America. All have played and continue to play a key role in the diets of people.

You can indeed see the world in a grain of rice.

こめつぶ

GRAIN OF RICE

The farmer plants a
Green shoot and then sees the world
In a grain of rice.

PASTA

PASTA &
GRAINS

RIBBON-CUT
Spaghetti
Capellini
Vermicelli
Linguine
Tagliatelle
Fettucine
Pappardelle
Bucatini
Lasagna
SMALL
Stelline
Ditaline
Orzo
Orrecchiette
Farfalle
TUBE-SHAPED
Fusilli
Macaroni
Zitti
Rigatoni
Penne
Canneloni
Conchiglie
STUFFED
Ravioli
Tortellini
Cappelletti
Agnolotti
Faggotini
Mezzalune
ASIAN
Egg Noodle
Flat Rice
Glass
Ramen
Soba
Udon
Shiritaki
Vermicelli
Lo Mein
Chow Mein
Rice Paper
GRAINS
RICE
Basmati
Jasmine
Wild
Uruchimai
Sticky
Sushi
Brown
Arborio
Valencia
Red
OTHER GRAINS
Cous Cous
Barley
Quinoa
Hominy Grits
Polenta
Freekeh
Oats

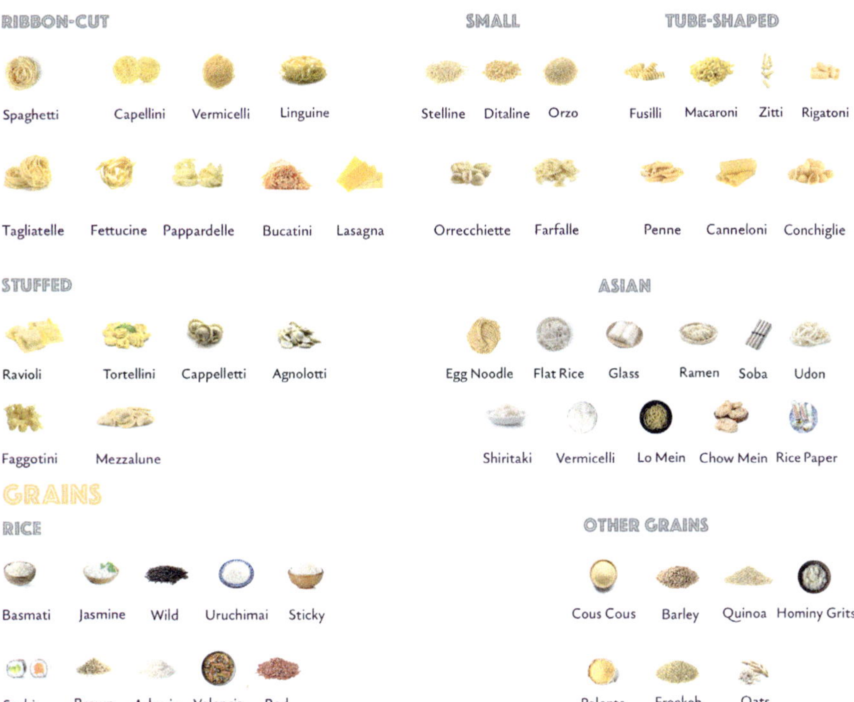

VEGETABLES

Eat your vegetables!

This admonishment to children is common around family dinner tables, as if vegetables are somehow a bad thing.

The flip side is that those who eat vegetables as part of a balanced diet are taken to task by vegetarians and vegans for whom eating anything other than vegetables is anathema.

The truth, of course, is somewhere in the middle.

What is more important is to have **fresh** *vegetables before the life and goodness are cooked out of them. And not processed!*

Frozen vegetables, however, are at once both nutritious and healthy. Not to mention inexpensive. Frozen baby spinach once microwaved is almost indistinguishable from fresh.

There are eight broad types of vegetables: FRUIT, BULB, ROOT, LEAFY, STEM, FLOWER, POD & SEED, and TUBER.

You are spoilt for choice and thus should vary the combinations. Eating vegetables makes sense for every meal.

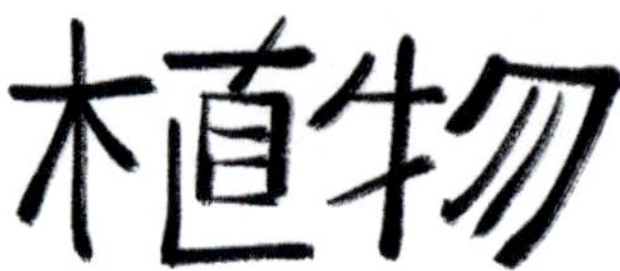

しょくぶつ

PLANTS

Have you ever thought
That some vegetarians
Actually hate plants?

VEGETABLES

FRUIT

Tomato Cucumber Aubergine Squash/Courgette

Avocado Pepper Corn

BULB

Onion Shallot Garlic Leek

Spring Onion Scallion Fennel

ROOT

Carrot Radish Turnip Beetroot

Horseradish Parsnip Celeriac Ginger

LEAFY

Spinach Cabbage Lettuce Bok Choy

Brussels Sprouts Kale Chard Cavolo Nero

STEM

Asparagus Celery Bamboo Shoots

Hearts of Palm Rhubarb

FLOWER

Cauliflower Broccoli Artichoke Capers

POD & SEED

Peas Beans Lentils Okra Green Beans

Chickpeas Peanuts Soybeans Licorice

TUBER

Potato Sweet Potato Yams Jerusalem Artichoke

SALAD GREENS

A meal at our house almost always includes a salad. Salads are greens, but they don't have to be green.

You can always get packaged salad: butter-head, baby spinach, lamb's lettuce, rosa verde... these are all good choices.

Or just buy fresh: bib lettuce, chicory (endive), romaine, gem lettuce. Or leaf lettuce. Or rocket. Or frisee, radicchio, watercress, or bak choi.

Or fennel.

Go off piste.

Try Shiso leaves. Pointed cabbage. Or Chinese cabbage. Or red cabbage. Flat leaf parsley for tabbouleh. And that old friend, the cucumber.

The possibilities are endless.

Just whatever you do, don't buy iceberg lettuce. This is not salad. This is cardboard pumped up with water.

And don't ever serve salad without some semblance of dressing, preferably without fresh garlic.

Get a salad spinner. This insures you will have crisp and fresh lettuce without being soaked

There is literally no excuse not to have tasty fresh greens every day.

あおな

GREENS

Why should you eat greens?
Because they're the colour of
The planet breathing.

Leaf Lettuce

Red & Green Butterhead

Baby Gem

Romaine

Red Endive

Belgian Endive (Chicory)

Lamb's Lettuce (Mache)

Rocket (Arugula)

Frisee

Radicchio

Watercress

Bok Choi

White Cabbage

Red Cabbage

Pointy Cabbage

Chinese Cabbage

Fennel

Shiso Leaf

Flat Leaf Parsley

Cucumber

PICKLES

A pickle.

Watch the young child's first reaction. A scrunched up face.

But they grow on you.

Indeed, the sour taste may become a craving (see old wive's tale about a pregnant woman.)

A pickle, no matter the cuisine, is the perfect foil to an otherwise overwhelming heavy taste or to spice up the bland.

In Japanese cuisine, pickles add both colour, texture, and taste to a bowl of rice. They are not seen just as an accompaniment, but an integral part of the dish.

Pickling, historically used to preserve vegetables, also stores up the positive nutrients. In Korea, pickled kimchi was the main source of vitamin C during long winters. Ditto sauerkraut or pickled gherkins in northern Europe.

Any kind of vegetable is fair game.

Pickled cabbage. Cucumber. Plum. Dates.

And pickling can be sour, sweet, salty, or all of the above.

Think chutneys, piccalilli.

Or a garnish. Pickled ginger or candied ginger are cousins, but their purpose is different.

So next time you think of getting yourself in a pickle, join the fine company of humans throughout the ages for whom this was both necessity and a pleasure.

つけもの

PICKLES

If you get yourself
In a pickle, perhaps you've
Done it on purpose.

Dill Pickles | Gherkins | Cournichons | Jalapeños | Guindillas

Pickled Vegetables | Branston Pickles | Picalilli | Sauerkraut | Kimchi

JAPANESE PICKLES

tsukemono

漬物

gari
Ginger|Rice Vinegar

takuan
Daikon|Bacteria

umeboshi
Plum| red shiso|salt

beni shoga
Ginger|Umezu

shibasuke
Cucumber|Aubergine|Red shiso

kyurizuke
Cucumber|Sugar|Salt

fukujinzuke
Vegetables|Sugar|Soy

SALAD DRESSINGS

Lettuce without a dressing is like going naked to a fancy dress ball. You may be talked about, but not in complimentary terms.

And salad dressings should be both complementary and complimentary.

They should be paired with the main dish (i.e. don't have a creamy dressing with a creamy stew, for instance).

Salad dressings (we always have salad either after or accompanying the main course) should be either palate cleansers, or a filling addendum.

A salad with crumbled blue cheese and a simple vinaigrette may be a palate cleanser; a full-on creamy Roquefort dressing is almost a meal in itself.

You will note the complete absence of garlic or raw onion. But I repeat myself. The presence of either in raw form is like the naked gate crasher. They will immediately dominate proceedings, but leave an after-taste that may come back to haunt you.

はだか

UNDRESSED

There are things which look
Good undressed but a salad
Is not one of them.

SALAD DRESSINGS

OIL BASED VINAIGRETTES

Vinaigrette

Dijon

Celery Salt

Lime Soy

Ponzu Rice

Black

Sherry

Lemon Sesame

Lemon Anchovy

Basil Pesto

Thai Dipping

Chinese Vinegar Soy

Yuzu Soy

CREAMY

Blue Cheese

Thousand Island

Ranch Dressing

Jalapeño

Dill Mustard Yoghurt

Caesar

Chipotle Cream

Green Goddess

Lime Coriander

Worcester Lime

Basil Pesto Cream

Tomato Anchovy

Soy Ponzu Yoghurt

Sriracha Creme

DAIRY & CHEESE

With all the best will in the world, and in spite of what doctors and other perhaps well-meaning folk suggest to save your arteries, dairy products (assuming you are not allergic) are what raise dishes from the mundane to the exceptional.

We have reduced the amount of butter drastically, replacing it nine times out of ten with olive oil. No cooking in butter, for instance, with the exception of pastry.

Cream is for special occasions or certain dishes, replaced by Greek Yoghurt.

Nonetheless dairy products are ubiquitous, in moderation.

Cheese is a key part of our diet.

Sunday mornings are toast with varied cheeses and meats.

A Mac and cheese is a perfect cold evening dish.

Cheese can be classed into six types: ***fresh****,* ***soft, semi-soft, semi-hard, hard****, and* ***blue****. Something for everybody.*

Cheese, in moderation is good for building strong bones.

No wonder the big boss is called the Big Cheese.

おおもの

THE BIG CHEESE

It's no accident
That the Big Cheese is also
Called Le Grand Fromage.

DAIRY & CHEESE

DAIRY

MILK

Milk

Single Cream

Double Cream

CREAM

Soured Cream

Creme Fraiche

BUTTER

Unsalted Butter

YOGHURT

Greek Yoghurt

CHEESE

FRESH

Cream, Cottage, Ricotta, Mascarpone

Queso Fresco, Feta, Mozzarella, Burrata

SOFT

Brie, Camembert, Chevre, Cambozola

Pont L'Eveque, Boursin, Pavé D'Affinois

SEMI-SOFT

Munster, Gouda, Havarti, Fontina

Jarlsberg, Taleggio, Reblochon

SEMI-HARD

Cheddar, Manchego, Comte, Gruyere

Halloumi, Monterey Jack, Provolone

HARD

Parmeggiano, Gran Padano, Pecorino, Romano

Caciocavallo, Asiago, Pepato

BLUE

Roquefort, Danish Blue, Stilton, Gorgonzola

Saint Augur, Dolcelatte, Cabrales

FRUITS

Glory is fleeting.

The perfect piece of fruit is on the cusp of ripening from a sour or bitter youth into a sweet and mellow adulthood. The taste which is fruity is the taste of mature fruits, picked young and ripened at leisure.

Fruits are possibly the healthiest things you can eat. They provide everything--roughage, vitamins, anti-oxidants, diuretics...you name it.

More to the point, they just plain taste good, giving you sweet, sour, bitter, and sometime umami in one go. They also add texture.

A few moments too long however, and the magic is lost.

Unless of course they are dried. Dried fruits are the perfect accompaniment to a cereal, muesli, or smoothie for breakfast.

But they are not the same as the ripe real thing. Enjoy that brief moment of perfection while you can.

人生の果物器

じんせいのくだものうつわ

LIFE'S FRUITBOWL

In your life's fruitbowl
Time will turn the bitter sweet
And ripe to rotten.

FRUITS

DRUPES (PITTED)

Plum Peach Apricot Nectarine

Cherries Olives Dates

BERRIES

Blackberries Blueberries Raspberries Redcurrants Strawberries

Grapes Cranberries Gooseberries Goji Berries Acai Berries

CITRUS

Orange Lemon Lime Tangerine

Mandarin Satsuma Grapefruit Kumquat

POMES

Apple Pear Quince

MELONS

Canteloupe Honeydew Watermelon

Casaba Pumpkin

TROPICAL

Avocado Coconut Banana Fig Guava Mango Papaya Pineapple Pomegranate Kiwi

NUTS & SEEDS

Nuts to you!

An epithet. But nuts are not a curse. Far from it.

Like fruit, they can be used in both sweet and savoury dishes.

They can be an alternative to flour. A snack. A topping.

An hors d'oeuvre.

They can be mixed and matched, and are used in almost every type of cuisine.

As for health value, nuts are a super food. They have low cholesterol, high anti-oxidants, low in carbs, and may aid weight loss. Nuts are a health marketing man's dream.

But somehow they are tarred with a negative brush. Just ask anyone who complains about being paid peanuts or has been called a nutter.

No matter. Nuts to and for you.

なっつとかじつ

Nuts and nuts

Ignore the bad press
Nutcase, paid peanuts, nutter-
Nuts are good for you.

Almonds	Brazil Nuts	Cashews	Pistachios	Pecans

Walnuts	Macadamia	Peanut	Hazlenut	Pine Nut

SEEDS

Sunflower	Flax	Pumpkin	Chia	Poppy	Sesame

BREAD

Give us each day our daily bread.

Think about what that means. For you to buy a fresh loaf of bread in the morning, a baker or factory somewhere is running in the middle of the night.

In the past, making bread was the first task of the day. A labour of love.

Even now having fresh bread is amongst the most pleasurable of sensations.

There are countless types of bread, ranging from those with yeast, or unleavened, sour-dough, or flat-bread. Every culture has its own variety.

Bread is a staple, but it can also be an essential accompaniment to any meal- breakfast,lunch, or dinner.

A buttery croissant. Toast with marmalade. A sandwich. The base for a pizza or a way to mop up sauces.

Wheat. Rye. Corn. Pumpernickel. Crunchy. Soft and chewy.

Learn to appreciate what bread does for you. Someone has been hard at work in the middle of the night giving you the pleasure of eating it.

ぱん

BREAD

With each day's sunrise
Baker's bread has already
Risen hours before.

BREAD

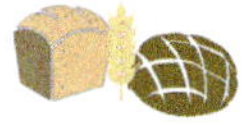

BREAD TYPES

YEAST

PASTRY/ SWEET

Brown · Wholewheat · Multigrain · White · Baguette · Ciabatta · Croissant · Pain au Chocolat · Brioche

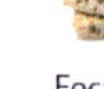

Pain de Campagne · Grissini · Challah · Focaccia · Bagel · Banana · Puff · Shortcrust · Filo

SOURDOUGH

UNLEAVENED

Sourdough · Pumpernickel · Boule · Danish Rye · Injera · Cornbread · Ryebread · Sodabread

FLATBREAD

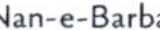

Pita · Pizza · Piada · Tortilla · Khobz · Bannock · Matzoh · Nan-e-Barbari

Naan · Chapati · Poori · Paratha · Roti · Dhosa · Papadom · Carta de Musica

ALCOHOL

Before, during and perhaps after practically every meal a drink is likely to be involved. Maybe just water, but perhaps an alcoholic beverage.

Not only that, but there is a good chance that alcohol will have been used in a sauce.

Drinks refresh, enhance the flavour of the food, and can give a glow of satisfaction.

In moderation. Never overload a dish, your stomach, or your mind with alcohol.

As Omar Khayyam said in ***The Rubaiyat,*** *wine can make something come from nothing.*

And if the Wine you drink, the Lips you press
End in the Nothing all things end in...yes
Then fancy while thou art, thou art what thou shalt be
Nothing.....thou shalt not be less.

さけ

SAKE

Sake should enhance
Taste and spirit; not make dull
Your mind and your tongue.

WINE

RED

Cabernet Sauvignon, Merlot, Malbec, Syrah/Shiraz, Zinfandel, Sangiovese, Nebbiolo, Carménere, Pinot Noir, Beaujolais

SPARKLING

Champagne, Prosecco

WHITE

Chardonnay, Sauvignon Blanc, Riesling, Viognier, Chenin Blanc, Semillon, Pinot Grigio, Albariño

ROSÉ

Grenache, Pinot Noir

FORTIFIED

Port, Sherry

RICE

Sake, Shaoxing

BEER

Lager, Pilsner, Bock, Dunkel, Pale Ale, IPA, Bitter, Brown Ale, Porter, Stout, Weissbier, Trappist, Special Brew, Japanese

SPIRITS

Whiskey, Bourbon, Gin, Vodka, Brandy, Rum, Tequila, Mezcal, Shochu

LIQUEURS

Grand Marnier, Amaretto, Pimm's, Baileys, Campari, Cinzano

WHITETIGER
FOOD DREAMS

SKILLS

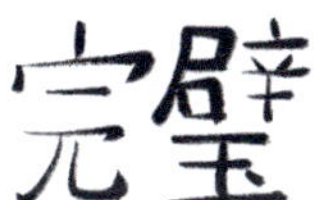

かんぺき

PERFECT

Never let it rest
Until your good is better
And your better best.

FAILURE SKILLS 

You might think it a strange place to start, a bit about ***failure*** as a skill.

But cooking is about trying, about experimenting, and ultimately about failing.

There is a difference between ***failing*** and ***failure***, encompassed in the following haiku.

失敗

しっぱい

FAILING

Failing ain't the same
As failure; failing's normal...
Failure...giving up.

As the writer Samuel Beckett put it:

Déja essayé. Déja échoué. Peu Importe. Essaie encore. Echoue encore. Echoue mieux.

Already tried. Already failed. No matter. Try again. Fail again. ***Fail better.***

Cooking is about failing better.

And learning how to learn from your failures is a skill, not only in cooking, but in life.

If it didn't work, pitch it and start over. Forget the defeat. Remember the lesson.

And you get to share your victories. The smile on someone eating your finished product is worth it all.

しょうり

WINNING

Winning has three steps:
Failure. Determination.
A satisfied smile.

KNIFE SKILLS 

SIX RULES REGARDING KNIVES

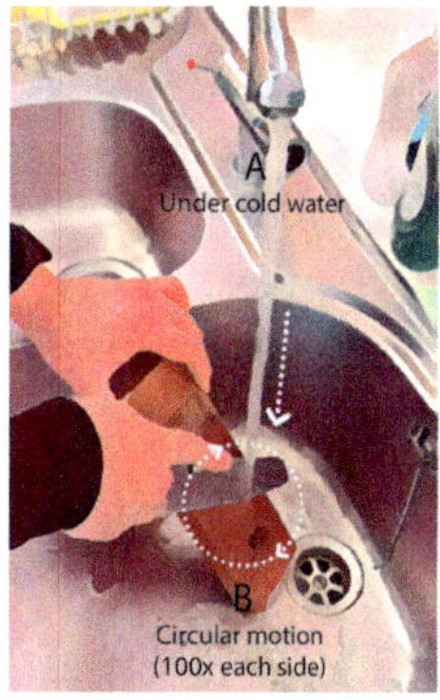

SHARPENING

1. *Buy the best knives. I use GLOBAL.*
2. *Always keep them sharp. At least once a month sharpen them up using a whetstone under cold water with a an angle tool which comes with the whetstone.*
3. *Always use a chopping board when you are cutting.*
4. *Use the tip of the knife as a fulcrum, rocking back and forth and taking advantage of the leverage of the knife to get a nice clean cut.*
5. *Feed using your fingers perpendicular to the surface you are cutting. That way if you mess up, you are talking a knuckle graze instead of an amputation*
6. ***Above all: PAY ATTENTION!***

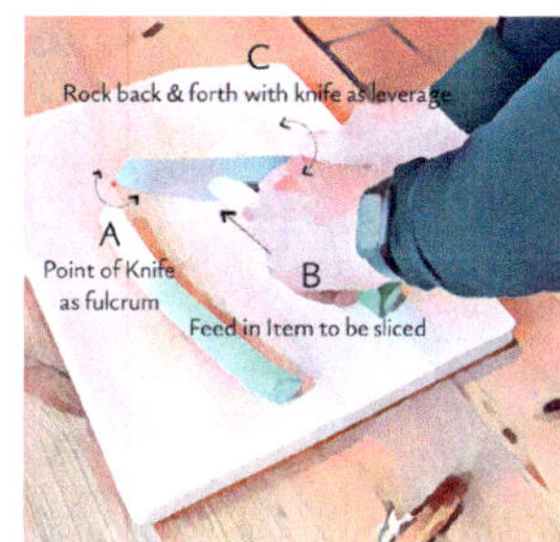

CUTTING

WHAT NOT TO DO.

1. *Don't store your knives in a drawer. These are instruments which deserve respect.*
2. *Don't saw, unless you are slicing bread with a knife with a serrated edge. A knife is a knife, not a saw.*
3. *Don't daydream (see point six above). A knife, after all, is a weapon.*

PREPARATION SKILLS 

1. Start before the beginning. Envisage the final product and then build the process.
2. Get all your ingredients lined up.
3. Spices and seasoning (i.e. salt and pepper) should be within easy reach. Roast and grind your spices.
4. Do the prep (the chef's word for chopping, slicing, mixing etc.) in advance, but not too far in advance. For instance, slice, dice or marinate the meat, prepare the sauce if appropriate, and chop the vegetables. You don't want them laying around gathering dust.
5. Lay the ingredients out in the order of cooking and cooking time in bowls, small bowls or ramekins.
6. Keep your workspace (chopping board and counter top) as clear as possible.
7. Practice to be quick, and clean up after each step as you go along.
8. When all is done, cook or assemble your product. Unlike building something, this may take a short or long time. Depends what you are doing, and what your heat source is.
9. Practice the end game.

PREPARATION IS ABOUT THINKING OF THINGS AS MUCH AS POSSIBLE IN ADVANCE. A CLEAN WORKSPACE INDICATES YOU PROBABLY UNDERSTAND WHAT YOU ARE DOING, OR YOU HAVE LEARNED THE HARD WAY. BY LAYING EVERYTHING OUT YOU WON'T FORGET THE NECESSARY THINGS.

ようい

PREPPING

Good preparation:
Start before the beginning
Practice the end game.

TASTING SKILLS

*The worst thing a person can say about food is that it is **under-seasoned.***

Seasoning basically means the addition of salt.

Why is this so important? Seasoning stimulates the taste buds and enhances the flavour of almost any ingredient (even sweet ones... think salted caramel). Under-seasoned food means the cook has not bothered to taste the dish. This is a cardinal sin.

*Tasting is a skill that begins with understanding the five tastes our tongue processes: sweet, salty, sour, bitter and umami, and how this happens. The first taste sensation as food hits the tip of tongue is salty (see graphic) but the key point is **balance**.*

And this only comes with practice in the long term, and with constant tasting with each dish. This has nothing to do with measuring out amounts of this or that. Taste is not about numbers. It is about sensation and memory.

*Oddly enough, spicy heat (i.e. chillies) is not a taste, though they are lumped in with bitter. **Capsicum**, the active agent in chillies, is a warning to the brain, not an taste invitation to identify and savour. Capsicum startles, numbs and then fades. Tastes linger in the memory.*

And think for a moment about pepper. Pepper is the yin to salt's yang. Cousins who always are lumped together but who get along famously.

Develop the skills to create and blend, to see what works with what and when, and how they balance. Too sweet. Too salty. Too bitter. Too sour. All are bad, and the only way to avoid is to taste constantly and adjust.

FIVE TASTES

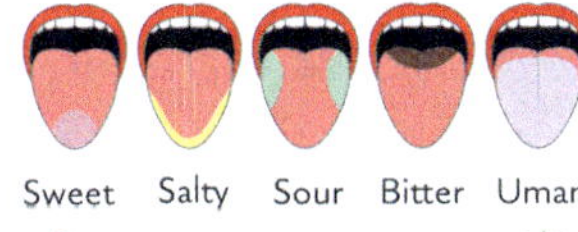

THE TASTING SPOON: THE MOST IMPORTANT PIECE OF EQUIPMENT

A PINCH OF SALT, A FEW GRINDS OF PEPPER

MIXING SKILLS

Just as important as tasting is learning how to mix.

Mixing is different than emulsifying or blending, though mixing is what happens when you do either.

Mixing is choosing what goes in order to get something out. Sweet or savoury. Sour or spicy. Salty or acidic. Umami.

What goes with what. How to roast and grind spices. What quantities and in what proportion. Wet or dry.

Surprisingly, the most unlikely bedfellows can be the most successful together in a dish.

Experiment. Never take no for an answer because you will never know until you try.

No cuisine has a monopoly on mixing tastes.

Traditionally you could use a whisk and a bowl.

However, get yourself a great mixer. The ***Cuisinart spice grinder*** *(pictured opposite) doubles as a blender. It is stainless steel, comes with two mixing cups, and is perfect for use all day long, from making your breakfast smoothie, to blending a marinade, to making a salad dressing or sauce. You can't do things in bulk, but cooking for two makes it a perfect tool.*

Throw in the spices, condiments, fruits, garlic, ginger, salt, pepper and olive oil into the mixer, whizz, dip a finger in and taste, and off you go.

MIXING IS MATCHING STRANGERS AND OLD FRIENDS

TIMING SKILLS 

Timing is everything.

There are essentially two types of timing in cooking: counting down and counting up. In other words, using a timer or a stopwatch.

The timer is the lazy way out. That is passive timing. The recipe might say 35 minutes, so you set the timer and wander off thinking that when the alarm sounds all will be hunky-dory. This is rarely the case.

Why? Because of that magic word: ***depends...***

The actual cooking time depends on the weather. The stove. Which shelf in the oven. What you are cooking. A whole host of factors. Timing is a guide. Nothing more.

The stopwatch lets you see how far along you have gone since you started. It FORCES you to pay attention, to check, and to make mid-course corrections.

Get yourself a watch with both functions.

And use it, whether or not it is a slow-cooked roast, a grilled steak, pasta, or a boiled egg. Timing is everything. The top chefs measure time in seconds which can make all the difference..

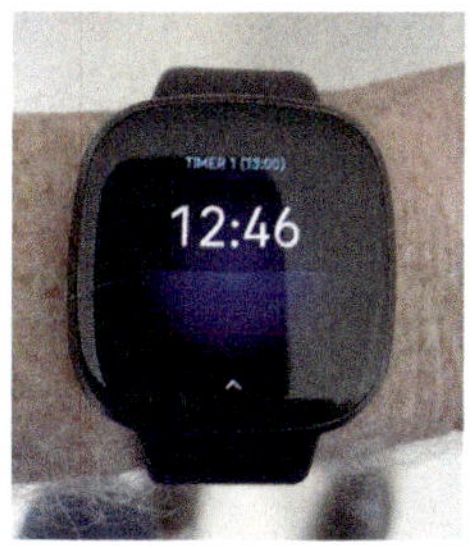

COUNTING DOWN- A TIMER

COUNTING UP- A STOPWATCH

IMAGING SKILLS

What makes us humans different from the rest of the animal kingdom?

*The answer is quite simple: our **imagination.***

Imagination is dreaming, conceiving of things that don't yet exist. The same is true of cooking. This is a cookbook, but it would be incredibly arrogant to believe that it is anything but suggestions -of ingredients, methods, tools, and things- to stimulate your own imagination.

Start to dream of what might taste good, and then give it a shot.

Bin the failures, both literally and figuratively, and remember the victories. Write them down, or take a picture.

Think of combination of tastes that might work. The sweet with the sour, the bitter with the salty, overlaid with an umami. Whatever.

Dream how you want things to look, and then paint your plates with the food you create.

Use your imagination.

そうぞう

IMAGINATION

Imagination
Is the free ticket which can
Take you anywhere.

PLATING SKILLS

In addition to eating, a plate of food should be a festival of eyes and mind.

We taste with our tongues, but we devour with our eyes. And a plate should draw the eater in, enticing him/her to want to have a taste.

The plate should be an explosion of colour and balance.

Each element of the dish should stand out yet blend in at the same time.

Don't just lob things on a plate. Arrange them with the star of the show proportionally bigger than the accompaniments. Center the elements

Choose bright colours to offset the duller ones. Mixed tomatoes. A sprig of parsley or coriander. A strategically-placed lime.

Be creative. It only takes a second, but the image can last a lifetime

More to the point, it is fun.

WHITETIGER
FOOD DREAMS

SCIENCE

科学と料理

かがくとりょうり

SCIENCE AND COOKING

Science can't create
Art but it sure as hell can
Ruin a good dish.

WHAT IS COOKING?

Cooking is the ***alteration*** of the ***molecular structure*** of a food by the ***transfer of heat*** or ***acid***.

1. The transfer of heat is through ***conduction*** (direct contact), ***convection*** (movement of air, water, or oil surrounding the food), or ***radiation*** (infrared or microwave).
2. The change in molecules is known as ***denaturation*** (muscle fibres, starch, sugars, and water) and affects the ***taste, colour, consistency***, and ***water content*** of the food.
3. The process of heat transfer is affected by ***time*** and ***temperature***.
4. Molecules change in different ways. ***Proteins*** coagulate; ***starches*** gelatinate; ***sugars*** caramelise; ***water*** evaporates; and ***fats*** melt.
5. These changes happen at ***key temperatures*** and can be good or destructive.
6. These molecular changes determine not only the ***taste, consistency, etc.*** but ultimately the ***pleasure*** of this food.
7. The cook manages this delicate process by choosing the ***method***, the ***timing***, and the ***application*** of complex scientific principles to produce a dish. A good cook intuitively understands change.

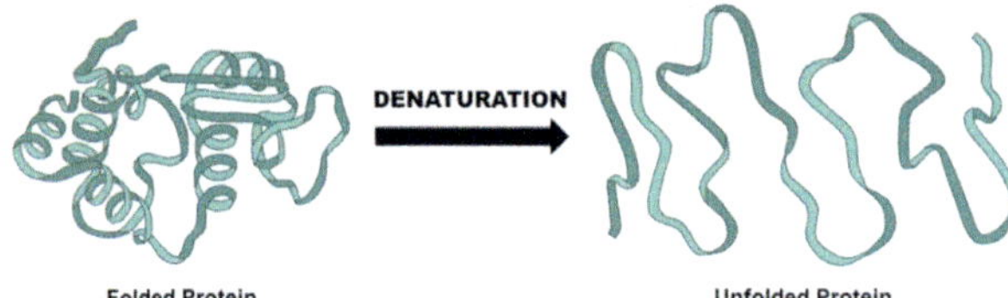

SOURCE: BLOG.THERMOWORKS.COM

Denaturation n. *The change in structure in protein molecules as a result of heat or acid.*

<u>Otherwise put, the molecules can no longer do their job. For want of a better term, they are ***cooked***. Not only that, but they ***taste and feel***</u>

TYPES OF HEAT 

Cooking is the ***transfer of heat*** from a source to the food being cooked.

There are basically three different methods how this occurs:

1. ***Conduction***- The heat is transferred by direct contact.

   Example of this is a pan on a hob.

2. ***Convection***- The heat transfers by the movement of a hot source around the food.

   This can be air, water, or oil. This movement of heat can be induced by temperature (like boiling water or hot oil) or mechanically (a fan-assisted oven).

3. ***Radiation***- The heat reaches the food via infrared or microwave radiation.

   Examples of this are microwave, hot coals on a barbeque, or a grill in an oven.

CONDUCTION- THE SLOWEST METHOD

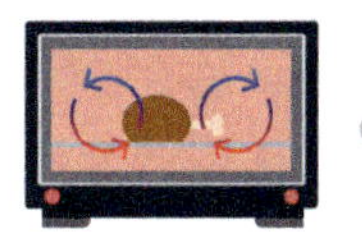
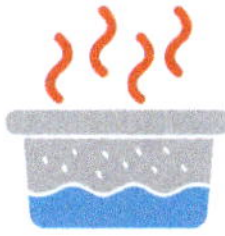

CONVECTION- THE MOST EVEN

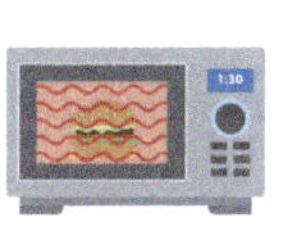

RADIATION- THE QUICKEST AND HOTTEST

TEMPERATURE AND TIME

*The most important scientific relationship in cooking is that between **temperature** and **time.***

*Basically the relationship is inversely proportional; i.e. the **higher** the temperature the **shorter** the time, and vice versa. Why is this important?*

For a myriad of reasons.

1. *There are key temperature points at which different molecules start to denature. The key proteins in meat, for instance, are **myosin** and **actin.** These affect the colour (pink), texture (chewy) and water content (juicy). Ideally, meat should be between* **50°-65°C** *(120°-150°F).*
2. *The speed at which these points are reached depends on the type of heat- conduction, convection, or radiation, all of which happen at different rates.*
3. *Once these points are reached and the molecules are completely denatured, take care not to exceed time or temperature or they will **overcook**,-(tough, brown, dry, burnt, or all of the above.)*
4. *On a more prosaic note, cooking also needs to kill off harmful **bacteria,** and this depends on what you are cooking, the key temperature point reached (***55°C** *- 131 °F), and how long you cook it.*

*The basic rule is: **Too fast or too high is wrong, and so is too short or too low.** Like anything else in life, you need to **pay attention.***

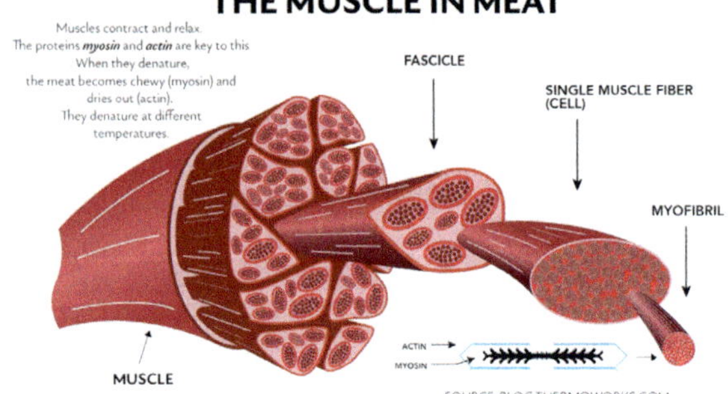

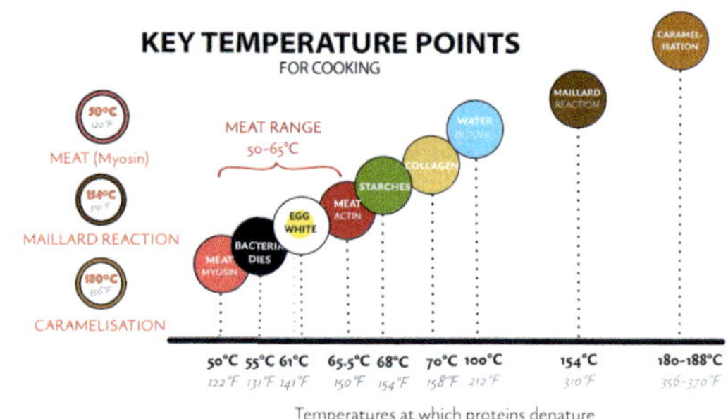

THE MAILLARD REACTION

You want your food cooked, but most of all you want your food to taste good.

And perhaps the biggest factor in achieving this is the ***Maillard Reaction****, the* ***browning*** *reaction in food which occurs with the application of heat.*

It is the seared steak, the crust on bread, the brown biscuit. It is the joy which hits our mouth. It is NOT however, the ***caramelisation*** *of sugar, since it is the change in amino acids and not sugar. The Maillard Reaction, named for the French chemist who discovered it, starts to occur at a temperature of* ***154°C*** *(310°F).*

In order for this reaction to happen several conditions must be met:

1. *The item must be* ***<u>dry</u>****. Too much moisture will create steam, and since water boils at 100°C, the required browning temperature will not be reached. Always pat meat with a paper towel before cooking.*
2. *The browning can occur quickly at a high temperature, or slowly over a long period at a lower temperature.*
3. *When browning meat, don't crowd the pan.*
4. *Brown first, stew later with meat. The brown bits are the tastiest.*
5. *Let pastry brown itself. Under no circumstances trade a pasty dough for a crisp brown. Be patient.*

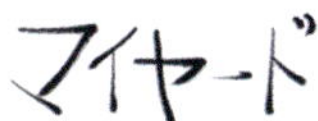

マイヤード

MAILLARD REACTION

Maillard reaction
Is the difference between
Pasty and tasty.

THE MAILLARD REACTION AT WORK

CARAMELISATION

Caramelisation, though similar to the Maillard Reaction is different. Same church, different pew.

Whereas Maillard is the ***change in amino acids*** which may be gradual to achieve the browning, caramelisation is the ***change in sugars*** which can occur quickly or slowly.

These sugars may be in different forms, i.e. pure sugar (think flan caramel) or the sugars found in starches in vegetables and fruits (think caramelised onions). Sugar fast. Starch slow.

This change finally is complete at a higher temperature than Maillard (***180°C*** (356°F) versus 154°C (310°F). The caramelisation of sugar is highly sensitive to temperature and can quickly carbonise beyond this point.

The two can be used in conjunction. For instance a stew which can be a combination of both the browning of the meat (Maillard) and the sweetness of caramelised onions and carrots (caramelisation).

Desserts such as crème caramel or sauces like ***dulce de leche*** or salted caramel sauce are made by gently boiling milk and sugar over a long period of time at a lower temperature (starting at 100°C).

MOLECULES PRODUCED BY CARAMELISATION

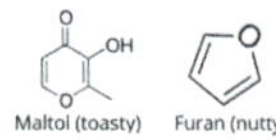

Diacetyl (buttery) Ethyl acetate (fruity)

At the temperature range caramelisation of sugar molecules creates new compounds with different distinct flavours

CARAMELISATION- SWEET & RICH

MEASUREMENTS

With the possible exception of baking, accurate measurements are the bane of any cook.

Recipes cross borders and countries and regions do their level best to complicate matters. Temperature and measurement differ from place to place.

That is why tasting is so important. But to help you along, get your mind into a single system (°C, kg/g and ml, for instance instead of °F, Oz, and cups). Teaspoons and Tablespoons seem to be universal, but there is a big difference between heaping and level..

Train yourself to know how much (roughly) something is, no matter what the measuring system.

*The key variables are **amount** and **proportion**. This book assumes everything is for two people, so some math is needed should you expand the number of mouths to feed.*

Ounces (oz)	Grams (g)
1/4	7
1/2	15
1	30
2	55
3	85
4	115
5	140
6	170
7	200
8	225
9	255
10	285
11	310
12	340
13	370
14	395
15	425
16	455

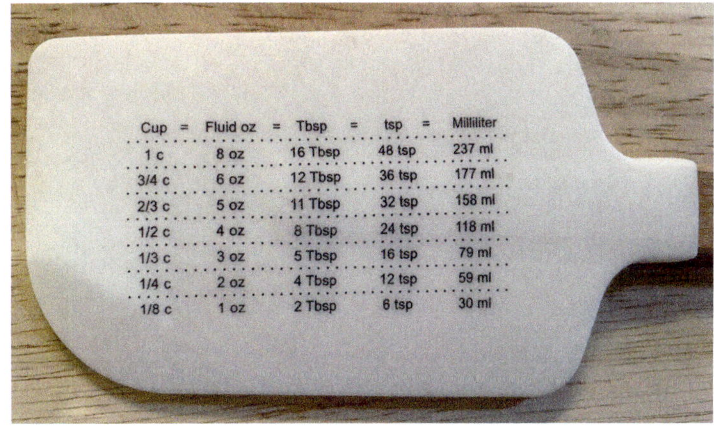

Cup	=	Fluid oz	=	Tbsp	=	tsp	=	Milliliter
1 c		8 oz		16 Tbsp		48 tsp		237 ml
3/4 c		6 oz		12 Tbsp		36 tsp		177 ml
2/3 c		5 oz		11 Tbsp		32 tsp		158 ml
1/2 c		4 oz		8 Tbsp		24 tsp		118 ml
1/3 c		3 oz		5 Tbsp		16 tsp		79 ml
1/4 c		2 oz		4 Tbsp		12 tsp		59 ml
1/8 c		1 oz		2 Tbsp		6 tsp		30 ml

QUICK MEASUREMENT FACTS

- *Litres to cups*: Half a litre is 500ml. 500ml is roughly 2 cups
- *Litres to Fluid Ounces:*500 ml is also 16 fluid ounces (oz)
- *Tsp to Tblsp:* A teaspoon is ⅓ of a tablespoon

CURING & PICKLING 

Cooking originally was a way of preventing spoilage of meat and vegetables for quick consumption by heating.

But it is not only heat which cooks. The denaturing of proteins and killing of harmful bacteria can also be achieved by other means, including sugar, salt, smoke or other acids.

This process is called curing or pickling, and there are many kinds and variations:

1. *Salt*
2. *Sugar*
3. *Nitrate or nitrite*
4. *Lime, vinegar or other acids*
5. *Smoking*
6. *Drying*
7. *Spicing*

All have a two-fold purpose, namely to preserve the food over time, and to enhance or impart taste.

Scientifically, the reason it works is that the various methods draw out water and make the food inhospitable for bacteria and pathogens.

PICKLING USING SALT, SUGAR, VINEGAR, & SPICES

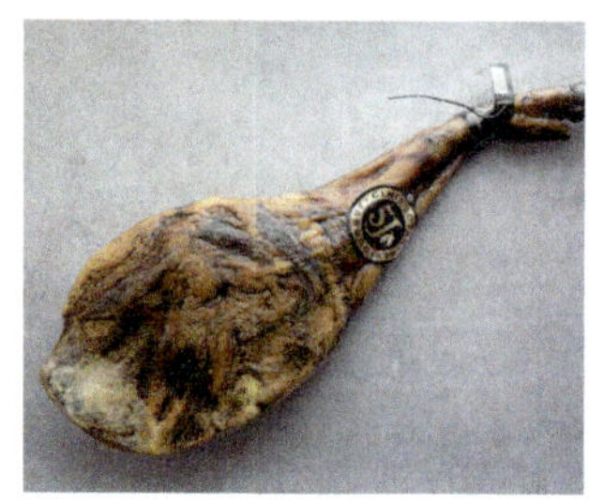

SMOKED IBERICO HAM

CRISP PASTRY

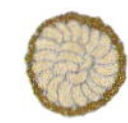

The perfect tarte crust is made of puff pastry which has been folded over in butter layers at least a dozen times (not your job, but the manufacturer).

Puff pastry rises and is crispy because as it bakes, ***steam created from the water in the dough and butter makes the dough rise up and pull apart*** to create that flaky, many-layered crunch.

The key to this is the marriage of ***cold pastry*** and ***hot oven***, with smooth edges and nothing to stop this steam from doing its work.

Therefore there are several rules to remember:

1. ***Thinner*** is better.
2. Lightly flour the worktop. Roll out the dough in the desired shape. ***Don't overwork*** the dough.
3. If you want the edges to rise, trace the rolled dough with only the weight of the knife inset from the edges.
4. Make sure the pastry is ***chilled and cold*** before cooking.
5. Make sure the oven is ***fully heated*** (**210°C**) before putting in the chilled pastry.
6. If you have a fan-assisted oven, put the pastry on a ***pizza pan*** (with holes in the bottom).
7. To cook ***blind bake*** for 15-20 minutes. This means using ceramic beads on foil to weigh down the dough (see photo).
8. Turn the pan around once after about 10 minutes to ensure an even cooking of the crust (the oven is hotter towards the back).
9. Before putting on your ***filling*** (which should have some thickener like corn starch in it so the juices will not run soggy), rub the cooked pastry with a stick of butter to create a thin film. Then put in your compote or fruit.
10. Turn down the heat to **170°C** and let this lower heat further crisp the crust. Bake for about 35-40 minutes checking colour of pastry.

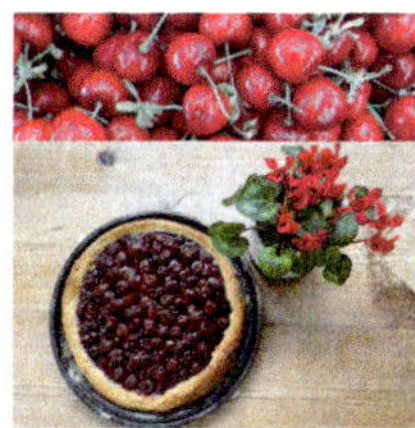

BLIND BAKE TO GOLDEN BROWN BEFORE FILLING

EMULSIFYING

They say that oil and water don't mix. When introduced, they shy away from each other like teenagers at their first ever party.

*That reluctance can be overcome, however, by the introduction of a third party. In cooking this is called an **emulsifier.** This could be egg yolks, mayonnaise (itself made with egg yolks), honey, mustard, tomato paste, garlic paste, or lecithin and other chemical additives. (Skip the last ones, mostly industrial). The unmixable molecules will get together if they are broken up into smaller bits and shaken.*

*There are three key elements to this dance: **agitation, time** and **temperature.***

How many times have you tried to whisk together ingredients (a hollandaise sauce, a salad dressing, a sauce) and have the elements split? This is not irretrievable, but it can be avoided.

Go back to the teenagers. If there is some teacher pushing them, it won't happen. There are a few basic rules to mixing:

1. *Get the chemistry right (i.e. the ratio of vinegar or acid to oil 1:4)*
2. *Always mix the **acid** and **emulsifier** first before thinking of adding any oil. (e.g. shake the vinegar, salt, and mustard in a vinaigrette).*
3. *Introduce the fat content (oil) in a steady stream. **Drizzle, don't pour**.*
4. *Whisk or shake vigorously but not too much. **Steady, tiger.***
5. *Don't overheat (e.g. make hollandaise over a **bain marie** - a bowl suspended over gently boiling water). **Easy does it**.*

EMULSIFYING IS KEY TO SAUCES

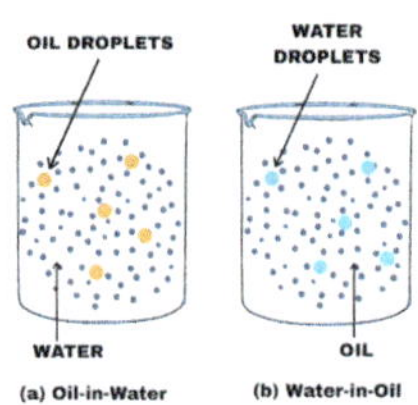

OIL AND WATER CAN MIX!

MAKING A SALAD DRESSING

Closely related to emulsifying, making a salad dressing is one of the simplest and yet somehow challenging tasks you can do, but it is critical to any salad.

There are essentially two types of dressing in this book: ***Oil/Acid based*** *and* ***Creamy.*** *This will concentrate on an* ***oil & vinegar dressing*** *or* ***vinaigrette****.*

A few pieces of advice.

Always use the best ingredients. Top quality vinegar. Good quality Extra Virgin Olive Oil. Sea salt. Freshly ground pepper.

And always go in the following order as per the picture.

1. *Acid and seasoning first. A finger of vinegar. A hefty pinch of salt (or perhaps celery salt). And 15 turns of a pepper mill. SHAKE thoroughly to mix BEFORE YOU ADD ANY OIL.*
2. *Add a finger of oil (Ratio of 1:1). SHAKE AGAIN.*
3. *Add more oil up to a ratio of 4:1, not all at once. SHAKE AGAIN*

Taste at each stage. Too acidic? Add more oil. Too salty? Add more oil. NEVER IN REVERSE.

Before dressing the salad ***at the last minute****, shake again.*

Job done.

THE THREE STEPS OF SALAD DRESSINGS

Always in the same order. 1) Acid & Seasoning first; Shake. 2) Oil 1:1; Shake. 3) Oil 4:1; Shake.

MAKING A CREAMY SALAD DRESSING

Making a creamy salad dressing follows the same principles as an oil and acid (vinegar or citrus) based dressing.

The order is

1. *Acid (lime,lemon, or vinegar)*
2. *Crumbled cheese (optional)*
3. *Mayo and Greek Yoghurt*
4. *Flavouring (Ketchup, chipotle, wasabi, mustard,celery salt, ponzu, soy sauce etc.)*
5. *Olive Oil (drizzled) and Season to taste*

Use a salad fork to blend to a creamy consistency at each step, tasting every time.

Perhaps one of the most important tools in your kitchen is the olive oil drizzler, a goose-necked bottle which you will constantly refill.

Being able to drizzle consistently is a key skill in making any dressing and sauce.

By the way, buy your olive oil in bulk. You will be refilling it a lot.

Mix well at each stage with a salad fork

MAKING A ROUX

A ***roux*** is a mixture of flour and oil or butter in order to make a thick paste. This can be used as a base for a cheese sauce for mac & cheese, for gravy or with milk for a bechamel sauce or stock for a velouté. Or even to thicken pie filling. Or make a croqueta.

Most recipes call for butter. ***THIS IS NOT NECESSARY***. I use olive oil, whether it is a savoury or sweet dish. Any fat will do. The science behind a roux is that the starch molecules absorb water and form lumps (gelatinisation), but heating and stirring the oil molecules allow the starches to make smaller clumps and bind into a smooth sauce.

Mix the roux ***before*** heating, using a silicone spoon to blend. Unless you want the roux to undergo a Maillard Reaction and turn brown (which will happen if you do not add the milk and continue to cook the roux), add milk just after turning on the heat.

The steps are:

1. ***One part oil*** to ***one part flour***.
2. Mix well until the flour and oil have completely blended.
3. The roux should be ***cooked***. It will change colour depending on how long you cook it and the purpose. For a bechamel or cheese sauce, faintly coloured (2-3 minutes), then blond (sauce or soup thickener-4-5 minutes), then brown (for meat gravies-5-6 minutes), then dark brown.
4. Have ready two cups or half a litre of ***milk***.
5. On a low heat, blend in milk, gradually at first, constantly stirring to make sure there are no lumps.
6. Gradually add ***flavouring*** (grated cheese, mustard, chilli paste, worcestershire sauce, seasoning, etc.). Taste as you go along.
7. Cook until all is melted and a smooth consistency, stirring often.
8. This base is versatile and can be saved fill out a pie filling (e.g. fish pie, with leeks, bacon, and spring onions) or in mac & cheese (pictured).

ONE PART OIL TO ONE PART FLOUR

A ROUX IS A BASE FOR ANY DISH WITH A SAUCE

(See MAC & CHEESE on page 100)

SAUSAGE-MAKING 

People always say that you are better off not knowing how a sausage is made.

Au contraire. The making of chorizo or a salami, for instance, must be undertaken with military precision according to specified measurements. Sausages are safe to eat because of the properties of salt, potassium nitrate, sodium nitrite, yeast, fat, spices, and (oh yes) meat, put together under sterile conditions in exact quantities and timing.

The combination of time, temperature, air, and patience result in a product which can be eaten immediately or cooked, depending on the moisture. It must be rigorously tested. The end product is a marvel of centuries of experience preserving meat, something which started with the cavemen and has evolved into an exact science.

WHAT GOES INTO A SAUSAGE

1. Ground meat and fat
2. Wine
3. Salt
4. Sodium Nitrite
5. Potassium nitrate
6. Dextrose
7. Bactoferm (yeast)
8. Spices (garlic powder, chili flakes, smoked paprika, black pepper, kampot pepper, oregano, thyme)

SOURCE: BRAY CURED MEATS

To know is to appreciate the craftsmanship and precision of the artisan.

INGREDIENTS-PRECISE MEASUREMENTS

ENVIRONMENT AND TIME

BOILING AN EGG

He/she doesn't even know how to boil an egg.

This throwaway insult would, if delved into further, disqualify most people in the kitchen, including chefs.

There as many ways of boiling an egg as there are opinions. The scientific formula, I kid you not, is the following.

$$t_{cooked} = \frac{M^{2/3} c \varrho^{1/3}}{K\pi^2 (4\pi/3)^{2/3}} \log_e \left[0.76 \times \frac{(T_{egg} - T_{water})}{(T_{yolk} - T_{water})} \right]$$

This formula, derived by the physics bods at the University of Exeter, basically says that it depends on the starting temperature of the egg. This assumes a standing start from cold water. It also depends on the size of the egg. Very large eggs may take 30 seconds longer.

SOFT-BOILED

From room temperature, the optimal time is ***3.5 minutes****. From the fridge,* ***4.5 minutes.***

HARD-BOILED

Take the cooking time for soft-boiled and double it. ***So 7 to 9 minutes****. Then plunge the egg into cold water and leave to rest for up to 17 minutes. Really?*

Also, once you boil the egg, if you don't plunge it into cold water, it continues to cook from the inside.

Not so simple, is it?

THE QUEST FOR THE PERFECT SOFT-BOILED EGG

COOKING RICE

It is hard to think of something so easy that people think is difficult as the simple act of cooking rice. However, because of crossing cultures, the methods (and indeed the raw materials) differ widely. This method works best with basmati rice, which will emerge fluffy with separated grains.

The science behind it? Grains of rice normally are 14% moisture. As they are in a heated liquid, they begin to absorb more moisture, up to a point. Too much water, the starch molecules burst and you get gloppy rice. Too little, they remain rock hard. The key is time and temperature.

In the absence of a rice cooker, there is a very simple foolproof method which requires very little input. Cooking ***risotto*** *is a whole separate category which requires constant attention, and thus will be treated elsewhere.*

COOKING ON A HOB (with heat diffuser)

1. *Put in desired amount of rice in a saucepan (roughly one cup/250ml per person)*
2. *Put in a good three-fingered pinch of salt*
3. *Fill the pan so that the level of the water from the top of the rice goes up to the first knuckle on your index finger.*
4. *Bring the rice to a boil on the hob.*
5. *Once boiling (keep an eye out), turn the heat to low and place a heat diffuser on the flame.*
6. *Cover. Don't peek. Wait 20 minutes and check.*
7. *Take off the heat. Let sit covered for a few minutes. Fluff up with a fork. DONE!*

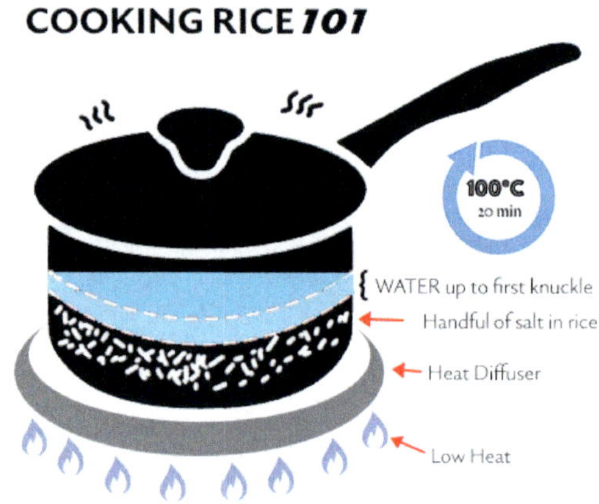

THE EASY WAY TO COOK RICE

MAKING RISOTTO

Risotto is an Italian creamy rice dish made with due care and attention. Though easy, it is not something to fire and forget for 20 minutes.

It also requires specialised rice, either ***arborio*** or ***carnaroli***. It is also emphatically NOT a one-pot wonder.

The steps are:

1. Gently sauté the ***sofritto***, the mixture of onions, carrots and celery (with the last two optional) in a frying pan. You may include anything else you want in the sofritto but make sure vegetables are ***al dente*** and meats Maillard-browned.
2. In a large saucepan, coat the rice (1cup or 250ml per person) in olive oil.
3. In a separate saucepan combine water, white wine, a boullion cube, and juice of1/2 lime. This is the ***brodo***, or broth. Keep to a gentle rolling boil. The ratio of brodo to rice is 3:1.
4. On the lowest heat for the main saucepan, ladle in one or two ladles of the brodo into the rice, constantly stirring. Start the clock. Continue ladling and stirring every minute or so.
5. After 15 minutes, put in the sofritto (along with whatever else you have sautéed- seafood, chorizo, vegetables etc). This may include the squid ink for ***risotto nero***.
6. After 18 minutes, fold in grated parmesan while constantly stirring and ladling all of the brodo until it evaporates.
7. After 25 minutes, check the consistency of the rice. It should be creamy, with a minor bite. It should NOT be mushly or hard. Serve with drizzled olive oil and parsley.

MAKING RISOTTO

Arborio rice+Brodo (broth)+ Sofritto

DEFINITIELY NOT A ONE-POT WONDER

MAKING A CARTOUCHE

*They say you can't fit a square peg in a round hole. The same is not true for a piece of paper cut into the form of a circle to make a **cartouche**.*

A cartouche is a circular paper lid used when you want to braise and glaze.

It is a classic French technique which keeps things moist while at the same time allowing caramelisation.

Making it seems like origami at first glance, but it is actually easy to do and there is absolutely no questions about the results.

Using greaseproof paper or baking parchment , you only need to follow eight steps to create from this square piece of paper a circular lid with a hole in the middle which will allow steam to escape and vegetables to caramelise, fruits to poach, meats to braise or soups and stews to thicken without forming a skin on top.

It should be de rigeur, for something so easy

You can fit this to almost any sized pan.

Dishes that can be made with a cartouche are glazed carrots, caramelised onions, or a tarte tatin.

Without the hole, the cartouche can be used to create a non-stick surface in a pan.

It is versatile, cheap, and effective.

Making a **CARTOUCHE**

BAKING PARCHMENT

PAN

1 Cut a square of parchment paper slightly larger than pan

2 Fold over from left

3 Fold up from Bottom

4 Fold Over from Right Corner

5 Fold Over from Right several times (like a paper airplane)

PAN

6 Measure the resulting triangle from the center of the pan to the INSIDE of the pan.

7 Cut edge and cut a tiny tip for a hole to let steam escape.

8 Unfold and ...

VOILA!

a paper lid for your pan.

RESURRECTION (LEFTOVERS)

One person's leftover is another person's starting point.

Rule Number One of leftovers: Almost nothing is irretrievable.

Take stale bread, for instance. The science behind it has to do with the levels of gluten and water in the bread. As with a tree, with age bread becomes brittle and dry as the starches crystallise and the water evaporates. Like a tree, old wood can be made into something useful.

The scenario. You've bought a load of sour-dough and haven't gotten around to eating it. There seems too much to chuck. The possibilities are endless not to waste it.

1. *If it is slightly stale, stick it into the microwave for 45 seconds and you will surprised to find it has found its former glory.*
2. *If properly stale but still cuttable, cut into small pieces, drizzle with olive oil and sea salt, and put it in a 170°C oven for a bit to create croutons or stuffing.*
3. *If it is really hard, soak it in water and use it make a vichyssoise or salmorejo or thicken a stew.*
4. *If it is really too hard, give it a good crack and feed it to the ducks in the park.*

As for other leftovers, before you bin them think: Can this sauce be used as base for a soup or some other dish; this chilli for nachos; this chicken for chicken salad?

Another good tip, if you are going to freeze stuff for future consumption, put it in an airtight plastic container with a label and a date. And be ruthless when you clean out the freezer. You should never have to carbon date leftovers. As the Japanese say: Luck is in the leftovers.

LABEL YOUR LEFTOVERS

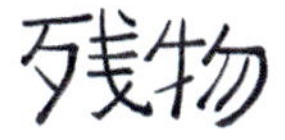

のこりもの

Leftovers

When you eat too much
You forget sometimes luck is
In the leftovers

WHITETIGER
FOOD DREAMS

COOKING METHODS

ほうほう

METHOD

There is a method
In your madness; it is called
How to cook a dish.

TYPES OF COOKING METHODS

Finally, to the section on cooking, which includes not cooking at all.

*Ultimately, the decision about what to prepare for dinner or lunch or even breakfast is a factor of several things. How much **time** you have? What **materials** do you have in your cupboard or fridge? **Who** are you cooking for? What do you **feel** like?*

*Or maybe, what have you **dreamt** about?*

These questions can be answered by the variety of cooking methods at your disposal.

<u>You will note that at NO TIME does this involve buying a ready made meal.</u>

1. *NO COOKING*
2. *FAST COOKING- Oven or Wok*
3. *MEDIUM COOKING*
4. *SLOW COOKING*
5. *COOKING MEATS*
6. *BRAISING*
7. *STEAMING*

THE METHOD FITS WHAT TIME AND MATERIALS YOU HAVE

NO COOKING 

Sometimes cooking does not involve cooking at all. .

*In fact, much of preparing food is about choice and assembly. It is about mixing ingredients. It is about **timing** and **freshness.** It is also about when you buy for each meal. But though there is no heat, is also about **temperature**, the ambient temperature in your kitchen, where you store your ingredients, and the season.*

A few questions to answer.

1. *What is the temperature of your fridge?*
2. *What is the current room temperature?*
3. *When do you buy salad and vegetables? How fresh is your produce? (Salad lasts 3-4 days in your fridge).*
4. *Do you use a salad spinner? Do you use other methods to refresh tired greens? (Like a bath in ice cold water, for instance.)*
5. *How far in advance do you assemble your meals?*
6. *What do you do when an avocado goes dark and mushy (i.e. when food is obviously past its sell-by date?)*

A few tips:

◊ *Buy produce fresh daily, where possible.*

◊ *Clean out your crisper drawer regularly. Don't use damaged goods. A dead leaf is a dead leaf.*

◊ *When you don't cook and are actually assembling, prep and service are one in the same. Allow a half an hour.*

CHECK THE TEMPERATURE OF YOUR FRIDGE AND KITCHEN

KEEP VEGGIES AND SALAD IN THE CRISPER

USE A SALAD SPINNER

FAST COOKING-OVEN  < 1/2 hour

One of the classic excuses for not cooking is ***time***, or rather the lack of it.

Fast cooking is cooking that takes roughly a ***half-an-hour or less***.

For proteins (i.e. meat) this could be a steak or hamburger (8-10 minutes), a duck breast (12 minutes), a Chicken Supreme (15 minutes), a poussin or pork chop (23 minutes), a rack of lamb (28minutes). For fish, considerably less (5-8 minutes).

The key fact is a high temperature in the oven (**220°C** 418°F). Also some sort of browning, usually in a pan which is also on a high heat on the hob (**210°C**).

The recipes in this book use one pan or one dish for fast oven cooking, either ceramic gratin dishes or white roasting pans.

The taste comes from the Maillard reaction in the initial browning. The high temperature cooking renders the fat, and keeps the meat moist while penetrating deep to the bone.

Because of the high temperature a stopwatch is needed. Too long or too short can be paid for in either blackened skin or insufficient cooking.

With ease comes vigillance.

FAST COOKING: BROWNING + HOT OVEN

ONE PAN COOKING- GRATINEE OR WHITE ROASTERS

FAST COOKING-WOK  < 1/2 hour

Perhaps the fastest cooking is in a wok. The concave nature of the pan and the thin gauge of the metal make this method the closest to getting directly onto the fire.

As such, cooking in a wok takes very little time in the actual cooking.

Which means that there are three key elements to remember using this method. ***Preparation. Preparation. And preparation.***

Not only must all your ingredients be prepared in advance, but everything must be within hand and in the ***right*** *order. This also applies to the tools you are using.*

A few quick rules:

1. *Make sure the wok is* ***screaming*** *hot. Smoking. This is high temp cooking.*
2. *Layer your cooking.*
3. *Make sure meats, even if marinated, have been patted dry. Maillard brown first as dry as possible. Take out and keep in glass bowl.*
4. *White or red onions and other harder vegetables (e.g. carrots) go next, along with chillies.*
5. *Starches (rice or noodles) follow. Use cold cooked rice for fried rice or blanched noodles.*
6. *Put in liquid flavour* ***at the end*** *(leftover marinade, or ponzu, soy sauce, wine etc.)*
7. *Scatter thinly-sliced spring onions or other seasoning only after the heat is off.*
8. *And most importantly, stir fry is what it says.* ***It is not stare fry.*** *Keep things moving at all times.*
9. *And don't be over enthusiastic about cleaning. You do not want a shiny wok. Wipe with an oily paper towel after cleaning each time to season.*

USE A WOK SKIMMER TO COOK AND KEEP THINGS MOVING

YOU DON'T WANT A SHINY WOK!

MEDIUM COOKING

Medium cooking does not mean average or mid. Basically it refers to temperature. Hotter than a Maillard reaction (154°C) and less than caramelisation (184°C).

That means things will brown over time, but they are less likely to burn as the sugars will not caramelise or char.

*This the optimal temperature is about **175°C** (350°F) in the oven (not fan-assisted).*

This means that the things will not cook as quickly (say 1hr instead of <30mins) but they will cook thoroughly. However, due care should be taken for the weight and moisture content of what is being cooked.

Take a roast chicken, for instance. A 1.5kg chicken at 175°C may take 1hr 15mins.

Roasting butter-nut squash at 175°C however, only 35-40.

The end result may be the same- a nicely browned and tasty Maillard surface, with the higher sugar content in vegetables and sheer size reducing the cooking time.

Medium heat is safer than cooking on low heat or high heat, less chance to under-cook or burn.

But is it better?

Not really. The main time I use 175°C is to finish off a tarte in the oven, or roast a chicken. Not all that often, to be honest.

So many recipes start off by saying, preheat the oven to medium heat, so there you have it.

ROAST CHICKEN-THE POSTER BOY FOR MEDIUM HEAT

SLOW COOKING

1 1/2- 3 1/2 hours

Think back on being presented a particularly tough problem in school.

The teacher urges you to take your time. Don't rush. Mull it over. Ponder. Break it down into smaller problems. Carefully consider all the possibilities. Sleep on it, even.

The answer might actually present itself over time..

*The same is true for **slow cooking**, which can be for either certain cuts of meat or liquids where lots of flavours need time to blend.*

Generally speaking, anything that has a large amount of collagen (the binding tissue) requires slow cooking. Brisket and Ribs for beef, for instance. Pork Shoulder. Lamb Shanks. Cheeks. This must all break down slowly. Tough becomes tender. Slow cooking is also important for liquid dishes. Stews. Ragus for pasta. Soups destined to be pureed.

Low and slow**. Low temperature for a long time. **140°C.

You can't forget, however, where the taste comes from. Before starting the slow cooking part, you need to Maillard brown at high heat, either in the oven or on the hob, and then place in a low oven or simmer on the hob, using a diffuser.

Just don't sweat it; solving tough questions always requires time.

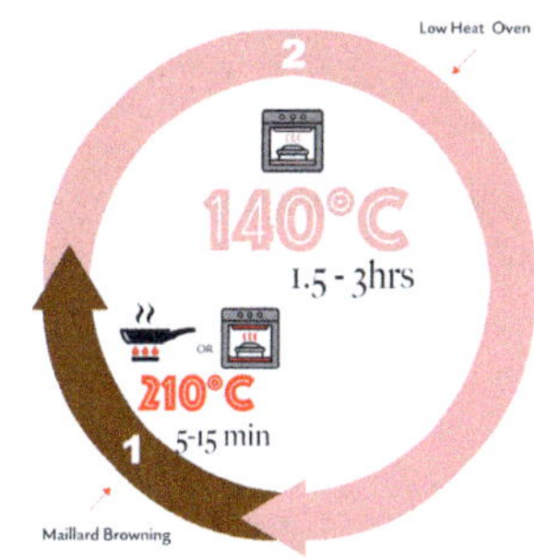

MAILLARD BROWNING, THEN LOW TEMP FOR LONG

FOR STEWS AND SOUPS,

LOW FLAME HOB WITH HEAT DIFFUSER

COOKING A STEAK

To sear or not to sear. That is the question, or rather questions.

Of course you should. But a cold sear? A hot sear? How thick the bark? Black or brown?

The center? As the French say: ***Bleu, Saignant, A point. Bien cuit*** (jamais jamais). Blue. Rare. Medium rare. Well done. Wean yourself off the desire to have well done. Steak ruined.

Perhaps just stick to the all-purpose ***medium rare***.

How long do you rest it? Five minutes won't hurt.

And what kind of steak? Filet mignon (overrated). Porterhouse. T-Bone. Sirloin. Ribeye. Tomahawk. Skirt. Flatiron. And how thick should it be?

And slicing it. Cross grain, or course. Thin is better.

The key rules to follow in my opinion are:

1. Wipe meat dry. with paper towel to have Maillard browning.
2. Hot griddle
3. Rub olive oil on meat. None in pan. Grind pepper. Salt ***just*** before cooking.
4. Press down with steel spatula or tongs.
5. Cook for desired time and flip. Bark should be browned. For sides, hold with tongs and press down to render fat..
6. Rest for the full amount (5 minutes is better.)

STEAK INTERNAL TEMPERATURES

BRAISING

Braising is a cross between boiling and roasting. It is a form of slow cooking, and can be done either on a hob (with a heat diffuser) or in a low heat oven (140°C). It basically means cooking something which is partially submerged in liquid in a covered dish.

You braise something which has a structure which needs to be broken down (i.e. the collagen or connective tissue in pork shoulder, pig cheeks, brisket, oxtail or short ribs). This will occur slowly and over several hours.

*A dish like **osso buco** (Veal or Pork shank with a bone in the center and bone marrow)) is a very good example.*

The steps are:

1. *Maillard brown the meat.*
2. *Remove and de-glaze the pan with liquid (wine or stock). This will scrape up all the Maillard particles in the pan where all the flavour is.*
3. *Put in the vegetables (onions, carrots, celery- otherwise known as a **mirepoix or sofritto** , but more about that later).*
4. *Partially cover with a liquid (wine, water, stock etc.).*
5. *Put in low oven (140°C) for a long period of time (2 hours).*
6. *Finish by removing the lid and broiling under high heat for five minutes (to crisp up the outside again).*

But this is not a recipe. This is a method of cooking. that results in moist, tender, and unbelievably flavourful dishes.

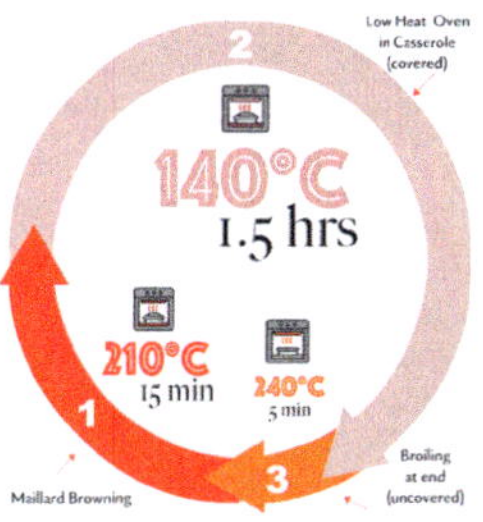

BRAISING, A HYBRID BETWEEN ROASTING AND BOILING

BRAISED OSSO BUCO

STEAMING 

Don't get all steamed up about it.

Steaming is a healthy alternative to other types of cooking because no oils are involved, there are no carcinogenic (read burnt) particles caused by fire or high heat and litle of the nutrients in the food (such as vegetables) are lost in the cooking process.

The downside to this is a lack of texture and flavour and the risk of overcooking.

Nothing is as discouraging is to be served a bland and mushy carrot or broccoli which has been steamed into submission.

There are roughly four methods for steaming:

1. *Suspended in a basket or colander over boiling water in a covered pan or wok*
2. *En papillote (A paper wrapping with water inside--say for fish)*
3. *A steaming basket*
4. *Microwaving*

To be honest, I rarely steam. Mostly clams, mussels, or crab. Or artichokes.

Occasionally broccoli if cooled and used with a dipping sauce. And of course dumplings.

But I don't get steamed up about it. Just make sure you salt the water and watch the time. 6-8 minutes max for carrots, half that for broccoli. 1-2 minutes for dumplings. 35-40 minutes for an artichoke.

GOOD CANDIDATES FOR STEAMING

FIT FOR PURPOSE

CLEANING UP & MAINTENANCE

清掃

せいそう

Cleaning

There is no time as
Valuable as that spent
Cleaning as you go.

CLEANING UP

Cleanliness is next to godliness. In the kitchen anyway.

It may seem an odd subject to include in a cookbook, but having the right tools and using them correctly to clean up before, during, and after cooking is not only desirable, but necessary. This is not just to make sure what you eat is safe, but to start each day and meal with a clean slate.

DO'S

1. Do have a hand-held brush. Change it often.
2. Do have the green scouring pads (not steel wool).
3. Do have ***Fairy liquid*** (or some facsimile) handy .
4. Do run everything under screaming hot water.
5. Do clean each plate before it goes in the dishwasher.
6. Do use ***Bartender's Friend*** to clear away grease and burnt parts of pans.
7. Don't cut corners. Stay with each task until finished.
8. Do use paper towels to dry unless you air dry on the rack and have time to do it.
9. Do wipe down all surfaces with a clean sponge. This includes countertops and the hob surround.
10. If your sponge smells, pitch it, or in a pinch boil it with detergent to kill off bacteria. But be ruthless when it comes to cleaning.
11. DO CLEAN UP AS YOU GO ALONG

DON'TS

1. Don't put off cleaning. Ever.
2. Don't use combo sponge/scouring pads. They are breeding grounds for bacteria.
3. Don't put things away wet.
4. Don't take shortcuts. Be thorough.

A clean kitchen inspires calmness and allows you to think and act clearly and efficiently. You will also enjoy your food knowiing you don't have a mess to deal with afterwards.

SCREAMING HOT WATER AND THE RIGHT TOOLS

MAINTENANCE

Good kitchen equipment is built for distance, not speed. If you maintain it well, some of it it can last...well...pretty much forever., or at least for your cooking career. If you don't maintain the equipment, however, it can degrade rapidly.

Take the picture of stainless steelware to the side. One pan is 42 years old. The other is five weeks. And lest you think I was born like this, Christina, my wife of 42 years, is the sole reason for the high standards and longevity, with uncompromising standards.

The same principle- buy good quality and maintain- is true for knives, for plates, for cutlery, and for the workhorses of your kitchen: pots, pans, and roasting tins. But only if you keep them spotlessly clean.

***Barkeeper's Friend** is a product which can restore the luster on most clapped-out and caked-on surfaces, within reason.*

Unfortunately, this principle is not true for all cooking items. Non-stick pans, old pans which won't work on induction hobs, or any piece of equipment that has moving parts and electricity perhaps won't make the cut..

Ovens grow old and deteriorate, especially if you haven't cleaned them.

Hobs get grimy. The electric sparkers wear out. Cleaning exhaust fans is almost a full-time job.

Nonetheless, if you want to cook, the art of cleaning and maintenance is not a luxury. It is an absolutely essential part. A dirty kitchen and disrcpected equipment is not a food dream...it is a food nightmare..

START EARLY AND CLEAN CONSISTENTLY

WHITETIGER
FOOD DREAMS

RECIPES

調理法

ちょうりほう

Recipes

Recipes are no
More than maps but it is so
Easy to get lost.

GUIDE TO RECIPE PAGE

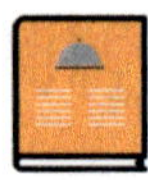

Each recipe page is one page only, divided into seven sections: On the opposite page is a picture, either including the process or just the finished dish.

1. The ***name*** of the dish and if necessary, a translation
2. A ***description***
3. Icons which represent the ***dish type, the type of cuisine, heat source, method and temperature***, total ***time*** to prepare, the basic ***food type, level of spice***, and degree of ***difficulty***
4. The ***ingredients***, including thumbnails
5. The ***tools*** needed, also with thumbnails
6. The ***steps***, divided into ***Prep, Cooking/Assembly***, and ***Plating***
7. ***Notes*** (which you can add yourself). These might be date done and any comments or improvements.

All of this information is used to categorise the dishes for easy retrieval or searching in the Index in the back of the book.

RECIPE TEMPLATE

❶ *NAME OF DISH*

Brief description/
Translation (if necessary)

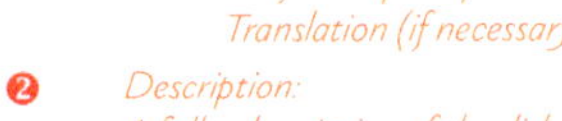

❷ *Description:*
A fuller description of the dish

❹ *Ingredients*

◊ List of ingredients

❺ *Tools*

◊ Necessary tools

❻ *Steps*

1. *Prep*
2. *Cooking/Assembly*
3. *Plating*

❼  *Notes*

Write your own notes: e.g.
Date done. Comments.
Improvements.
Change in ingredients etc.

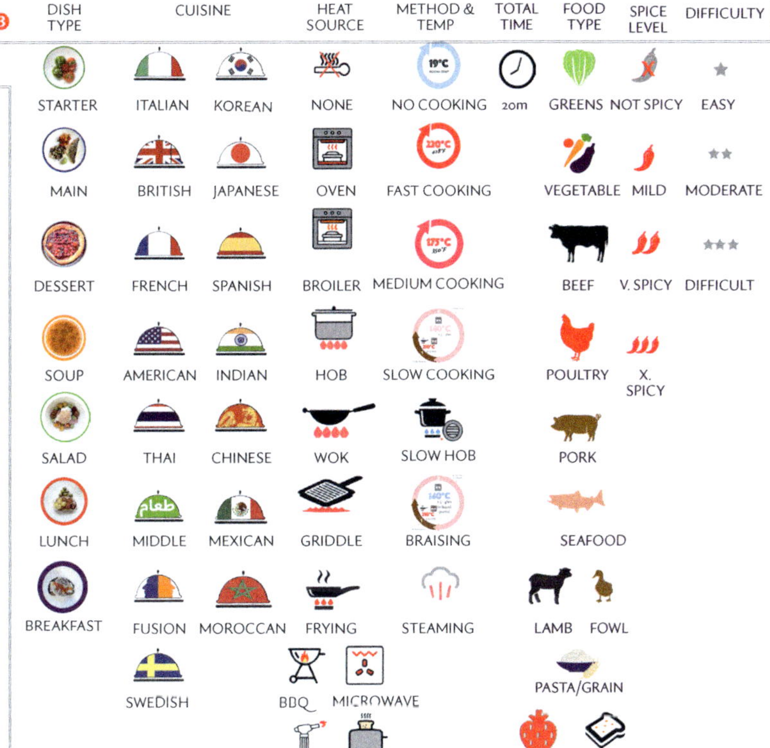

WHITETIGER
FOOD DREAMS

FAVOURITES

好物

こうぶつ

FAVOURITE

A favourite is
No more than the memory
Of a dream come true.

SPAGHETTI FALSI DI CETRIOLI

Fake Cucumber Spaghetti

 STARTER |  ITALIAN |  HEAT SOURCE |  NO COOKING |  2om |  SALAD |  NOT SPICY |  EASY

Description:

A trompe l'oeil salad of cucumber (cetrioli), tomatoes, roasted red peppers, and parmesan which tricks the mind into thinking...just another plate of spaghetti.

Ingredients

- Long Cucumber x 2
- Packet of Tomatoes (cherry or santini)
- 1/2 jar piquillo or red peppers
- Lime x 1
- Peperoncino Paste (1 teaspoon)
- Parmesan or Padano
- Extra Virgin Olive Oil
- Maldon Sea Salt
- Ground Pepper
- Optional Sour-dough toast
- Optional A good French cheese

Tools

- Julienne slicer
- CUISINART spice grinder

Steps

Prep: Peel and cut the cucumbers lengthwise into two halves. Using the scoop on your julienne slicer (or a spoon) scrape out the seeds. Then dry with a paper towel. Julienne the cucumber lengthwise using the julienne slicer and create little spaghetti strands of cucumber. Put in paper towel and squeeze as much moisture out as possible. Place in a glass bowl and add sea salt and olive oil

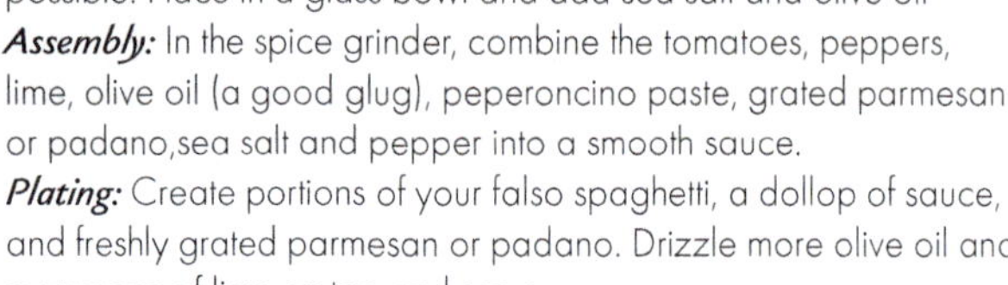

Assembly: In the spice grinder, combine the tomatoes, peppers, lime, olive oil (a good glug), peperoncino paste, grated parmesan or padano,sea salt and pepper into a smooth sauce.

Plating: Create portions of your falso spaghetti, a dollop of sauce, and freshly grated parmesan or padano. Drizzle more olive oil and a squeeze of lime on top and serve.

This can be either a starter or a light supper, especially with added toast and cheese.

Notes

SPAGHETTI FALSI DI CETRIOLI

MAC & CHEESE

Sharp and spicy macaroni

MAIN BRITISH HOB OVEN FAST COOKING 45m PASTA/GRAIN MILD EASY

Description:
A classic dish with a slight twist of spice: chilli cheddar, English mustard, Frank's Hot Sauce, baby leeks, and smoked bacon

Ingredients

- Macaroni
- Cheddar Cheese
- Chilli Cheddar
- Baby Leeks
- Smoked Back Rasher Bacon
- Frank's Hot Sauce
- Coleman's English Mustard
- Worcestershire Sauce
- Olive Oil
- Milk
- Flour
- Salt & Pepper
- Chilli Flakes
- Splash of white wine

Tools

- Saucepans
- Ceramic Casserole
- Knife
- Silicone Spoon

Steps

Prep: Dice the baby leeks and bacon. Cut the cheese into manageable slices. Preheat oven to **180C** (356°F).

Cooking: Boil the pasta for 7-9 minutes. Fry the bacon until nicely browned. Sauté the leeks in the bacon fat. Finish with a splash of white wine. Make a roux (See MAKING A ROUX on page 71) with the olive oil and flour, gradually adding milk and cheese while stirring. Blend in mustard, hot sauce, worcestershire sauce and season to taste. Drain macaroni and put in casserole with olive oil drizzled on bottom. Mix in bacon, leeks, and cheese sauce. Top with grated cheddar and parmesan.

Bake at **180°C** for 25min, **220°C** for 5 minutes.

Plating: Serve in pasta bowl and drizzle with olive oil accompanied by a salad.

Hearty, rich, and eminently leftover-able..

Notes

MAC & CHEESE

RISOTTO NERO FRUTTI DI MARE

Black Squid ink risotto with shrimps, mussels & scallops

MAIN

ITALIAN

HOB

FAST COOKING

45m

PASTA/GRAIN

NOT SPICY

EASY

Description:

A flavourful easy dish which sings of the sea and a crystalline Sardinian sky

Ingredients

- Arborio rice
- Shrimp
- Mussels
- Scallops
- Clove of Garlic
- Spring Onions
- Chicken Boullion cube
- Black Squid Ink
- White Wine
- Lime
- Parmesan (freshly grated)
- Seasoning
- Flat leaf parsley

Tools

- Saucepans
- Silicone Spoon
- Ladle

Steps

Prep: Get two saucepans and a frying pan. Slice the spring onions, separating white parts from green. Wash the mussels. In a pestle and mortar, create a paste of ½ lime, one clove garlic, olive oil, and sea salt.

Cooking: To make the ***sofritto*** sauté the onions, shrimps and mussels in olive oil for several minutes, and put in the garlic paste and a splash of white wine and stir. In one saucepan make the ***brodo*** with 500ml water, 500ml white wine, one chicken bouillon cube and juice of ½ lime and bring to gentle boil. In the main saucepan, coat 500ml of rice in oil and heat along with the whites of spring onions. Over low heat, gradually ladle in the brodo while stirring constantly for 15 minutes, after which add in the squid ink. At 18 minutes, put in the grated parmesan and ***sofritto*** and stir. After 25 minutes, check consistency of rice and season to taste. It should be creamy and the rice should be cooked through. Blend in olive oil. Pat dry scallops. Lightly oil a frying pan. Sauté scallops (1-2 minutes) on high heat until browned. Season. (See MAKING RISOTTO on page 75)

Plating: Serve in pasta bowl. Arrange scallops on top, scatter parsley and drizzle with olive oil accompanied by a salad.

A whiff of the Mediterranean even in the depths of winter.

Notes

RISOTTO NERO FRUTTI DI MARE

CHORIZO KALAMATA TAGLIATELLE

A hispano-greco-italian jumble of deliciousness

MAIN

FUSION

HOB

SLOW COOKING

1.5hr

PASTA/GRAIN

V. SPICY

EASY

Description:
Okay so an Italian would baulk at the chorizo and wonder why Greek olives were necessary. Because the combo tastes delicious, that's why. The trifecta of tomatoes

Ingredients

- Chorizo (picante) x 6
- Pitted Kalamata olives (1 jar)
- Spring onions x 4
- Baby tomatoes (1 punnet)
- Tinned tomatoes x 1 (MUTTI)
- Tomato Paste (1 tblsp)
- Peperoncino paste (1 tblsp)
- Red wine (Glug)
- Olive Oil
- Sea Salt and Black Pepper
- Chilli flakes
- Brown sugar (1 tsp)
- Parmesan
- Flat leaf parsley
- Romaine lettuce
- Radishes
- Lemon (for vinaigrette)

Tools

- Saucepan with cover
- Silicone Spoon
- Heat diffuser
- Colander
- Glass Bowl
-

Steps

Prep: Slice chorizo into bite size chucks. Slice spring onions and halve the baby tomatoes.

Cooking: Maillard brown the chorizo over a hot flame in the deep frying pan. Then chuck in the spring onion and stir fry for 1-2 minutes. Add kalamata olives (drained), tomatoes, tinned tomatoes, chilli flakes, peperoncino paste and tomato paste. Finish with a glug of red wine and a healthy drizzle of olive oil. Season with a pinch of salt and a bit of black pepper. Put onto heat diffuser on low heat, cover and cook for 1 hour 20 minutes at a gradual boil, stirring every so often. Taste and add sugar or wine to temper the spiciness. Boil tagliatelle in large saucepan of salted water as per the packet (usually 8-10 minutes). Drain and drizzle with olive oil.

Plating: Serve in pasta bowl. Top with freshly grated parmesan, scatter parsley and drizzle with olive oil accompanied by a salad of romaine and radishes and a lemon vinaigrette (See MAKING A SALAD DRESSING on page 69).

After all Mediterranean peoples are different pews of the same church of sun, sea and varieties of similar products. Is this fusion? Or just a logical marriage of cousins..

Notes

CHORIZO KALAMATA TAGLIATELLE

MUSHROOM STROGANOFF

Simple fresh ingredients from the forest floor

MAIN

FUSION

HOB

FAST COOKING

45m PASTA

VEGETABLE

NOT SPICY

EASY

Description:

A rich easy dish that at once is filling and meaty without any meat and without being heavy. Good the next day or beyond, on toast or as a reprise.

Ingredients

- ◊ White mushrooms x 1
- ◊ Chestnut mushrooms x 1
- ◊ Spring Onions
- ◊ Smoked Paprika (1 tsp)
- ◊ Lime x 1
- ◊ Ponzu (glug)
- ◊ Worcestershire sauce (1 tsp)
- ◊ Red wine (good glug)
- ◊ Sour cream (small)
- ◊ Tomato Paste (1 tblsp)
- ◊ Peperoncino paste (1tsp)
- ◊ Rocket
- ◊ Cornstarch or flour (for thickening)
- ◊ Tagliatelle
- ◊ Sea Salt and Back Pepper
- ◊ Olive Oil

Tools

- ◊ Knife
- ◊ Deep Frying pan with lid
- ◊ Glass Bowls
- ◊ Silicone Spoon

Steps

Prep: Slice mushrooms. Slice Spring onions. Finely chop rocket.

Cooking: Season and then sauté mushrooms for five minutes until browned in a light amount of olive oil. Toss often. Add spring onions (2 minutes). Grate lime zest and add along with smoked paprika, peperoncino and tomato paste. Add red wine and ponzu and juice of ½ lime. Let simmer on low heat for 20 minutes with lid. Remove lid, increase heat to medium, and add sour cream and stir while sauce reduces (10 minutes). Thicken before serving if needed by dissolving flour or corn starch in a small jar, shaking thoroughly and adding to sauce while stirring. Boil tagliatelle in salted water as per instructions (2-3 minutes for fresh, 8-10 minutes for dried). Drain in colander and mix with a drizzle of olive oil.

Plating: Serve on top of tagliatelle in pasta bowl. Scatter finely chopped rocket on top and drizzle with olive oil accompanied by a salad.

*An old family favourite. We'll call it fusion as in **con**fusion, as the provenance of this dish is claimed by many cultures. Russian. French. British. You name it.*

Notes

MUSHROOM
STROGANOFF

WHITETIGER
FOOD DREAMS

STARTERS, SMALL PLATES & SIDES

FISH MEDLEY

A seasonal version of the traditional smoked salmon

STARTER

BRITISH

HEAT SOURCE

NO COOKING

10m

SALAD

NOT SPICY

EASY

Description:

Smoked salmon as a starter. Hohum... But not when you pair it with two types of anchovies, capers, taramasalata, lamb's lettuce, and a citrus salad dressing, anything but. More like a HoHo!

Ingredients

- Smoked Salmon
- Capers (small)
- Taramasalata
- Ortiz or other high quality anchovies
- Boquerones (Anchovies in vinegar)
- Lamb's lettuce

For the dressing:

- Lime
- Yuzu
- Sea Salt and Black Pepper
- Olive Oil

Tools

- Chef's Knife (sharp)
- Squeeze bottle

Steps

Prep: Using a template, slice smoked salmon into the shape of a Christmas tree (or any other suitable shape). Put taramasalata into a plastic bag to use as piping.

Assembly: Arrange Anchovies as alternate rows of tinsel on the smoked salmon tree. Squeeze droplets of taramasalata and capers as ornaments. Toss lamb's lettuce. Make a Yuzu/Lime dressing (See MAKING A SALAD DRESSING on page 69)

Forming the smoked salmon into a Christmas tree shape adds a nice touch to this small plate, which of course is not necessary the rest of the year.

Notes

CHRISTMAS FISH MEDLEY

KOREAN SCALLION SEAFOOD PANCAKES

Crispy on the outside, soft on the inside Korean masterpiece

 STARTER  KOREAN  FRYING  FAST COOKING  20m  SEAFOOD  MILD ★★ MODERATE

Description:

*These pancakes owe their crispness to a 1:1 mixture of the pancake flour and ice-cold carbonated water (Sodastream home-made or Perrier). They can be accompanied by store-bought gyoza or shumai (pictured) and blanched Broccoli with **4 different dipping sauces***

Ingredients

- ◊ Korean pancake flour (from Asian food store)
- ◊ Ice-cold Carbonated water
- ◊ Miso paste (1 tblsp)
- ◊ Spring Onions
- ◊ Shrimp
- ◊ Chilli Pepper x 1
- ◊ Broccoli spears
- ◊ Gyoza or Shumai (store-bought)

Sauces (mix all but Sauce#4 in spice grinder)

- ◊ ***Sauce #1***: Dark Soy sauce
- ◊ Rice Vinegar
- ◊ Chilli flakes
- ◊ ***Sauce #2:*** Mayonnaise (1 tblsp)
- ◊ Greek Yoghurt (1 tblsp)
- ◊ Wasabi from tube
- ◊ Ponzu (1 tblsp)
- ◊ ***Sauce #3:*** Red Peppers from Jar x 2
- ◊ Lime x 1
- ◊ Olive Oil
- ◊ Sea Salt and Black Pepper
- ◊ ***Sauce #4:*** Ponzu and olive oil

Tools

- ◊ Saucepan
- ◊ Small non-stick frying pan
- ◊ Spice grinder
- ◊ Glass Bowls x 2
- ◊ Ladle
- ◊ Spatula
- ◊ Digital Thermometer

Steps

Prep: Chop shrimps, finely slice chillies, and slice spring onions lengthwise into batons. Make each sauce in the spice mixer and put in ramekins. Blanch broccoli spears in boiling salted water in saucepan and run under cold water in colander. Mix batter in glass bowl at last moment with equal parts 1:1 of Korean pancake batter,ice-cold carbonated water (should fizz up) and miso. Blend in shrimp, chillies, and spring onions. ***Cooking:*** Put 2cm of vegetable oil in the frying pan and under high heat bring to 175°C. Ladle batter and flatten with spoon. Fry 3-4 minutes ***until crisp*** and flip carefully. Each pancake should be dark golden. Crispiness is key. Drain on paper towel and if you are cooking in batches, keep in oven. Steam fry, or microwave the gyoza or shumai for 1 minute. ***Plating:*** Cut into finger food sizes and plate with the shumai and gyoza with the dipping sauces handy and the broccoli to the side.

Savour each bite. Might sound like overkill with the four sauces, but you will want this to last forever.

Notes

파전
PAJEON
KOREAN SCALLION PANCAKES
SHRIMP | BROCCOLI SPEARS

CHICKEN WINGS

Wings with crudités and roquefort dip

STARTER | AMERICAN | HOB | OVEN | FAST COOKING | 30m | POULTRY | MILD | EASY

Description:

Any dish whose main flavour is by a guy named Frank has got to be American, even though the cheese used is French. And there is no reason not to have this for dinner.

Ingredients

- Chicken wings, either whole or already cut
- Spring Onions
- Lime x 1
- Frank's Hot Sauce
- Olive Oil
- Sea Salt and Black Pepper
- Chilli Flakes
- White wine

Roquefort Dressing

- Roquefort cheese (Crumbled)
- Mayonnaise (1 tblsp)
- Greek Yoghurt (1 tblsp)
- Red Wine Vinegar (1 tsp)
- Celery Salt
- Pepper
- Olive Oil

Tools

- Frying Pan
- Roasting tin
- Poultry Shears
- Silicone brush
- Steps

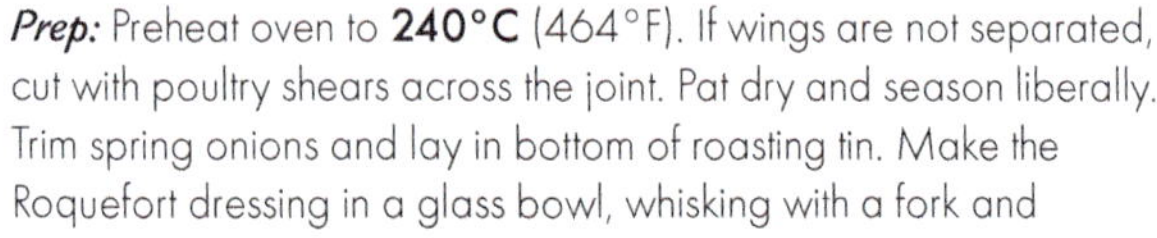

Prep: Preheat oven to **240°C** (464°F). If wings are not separated, cut with poultry shears across the joint. Pat dry and season liberally. Trim spring onions and lay in bottom of roasting tin. Make the Roquefort dressing in a glass bowl, whisking with a fork and then transfer to ramekins. (See MAKING A CREAMY SALAD DRESSING on page 70) Trim, peel, and cut carrots and celery into batons.

Cooking: In hot skillet with a film of olive oil, Maillard brown the wings in batches. When browned, place skin side up in roasting tin on top of the onions. Squeeze one lime, add numerous glugs of Frank's Hot Sauce, and paint on all sides with the silicon brush. Season again, season, sprinkle some chilli flakes, and drizzle olive oil. Set your stopwatch. Bake at **240°C** for **23 minutes**. At 13 min turn over wings and baste. Put in a glug of white wine. At the end of 23 minutes, if not browned enough, turn on broiler for a few minutes. When you take them out, make sure the liquid coats them evenly and let cool a few minutes.

Plating: Arrange finished wings on a plate, with the ramekins of Roquefort dressing and the crudités in a small bowl.

A perfect quick mid-week supper whose cost is negligible (a pack of chicken wings is appr.£1.70). Leftovers are great the next day.

Notes

CHICKEN WINGS | CRUDITÉS
CREAMY ROQUEFORT

TORTILLA

Spanish Classic-pleasure without pain

STARTER

SPANISH

HOB

BROILER

FAST COOKING

20m
PORK

NOT SPICY

EASY

Description:

Either as a small dish or a light supper, a tortilla is quick and very tasty. The Spanish purist will disagree with this adaptation, but all is fair in love and cooking.

Ingredients

- Eggs x 4
- Baby Potatoes
- Lardons
- Manzanilla Olives
- Spring Onions
- Dijon Mustard
- Pimentón (Smoked Paprika)
- Greek Yoghurt
- Cheddar
- Parmesan
- Olive Oil
- Sea Salt and Black Pepper

Tools

- Knife
- Small non-stick frying pan
- Spatula
- Glass bowl

Steps

Prep: Preheat oven to broil (**240°C**). Crack and whisk eggs with yoghurt, sea salt pepper, pimentón (smoked paprika)and mustard. Cube and boil small potatoes for 8-10. Halve olives. Grate cheddar and parmesan. Fry lardons until crisp. Mix all ingredients in a glass bowl thoroughly with a fork.

Cooking: Lightly drizzle olive oil in small pan and pour in mixture. Grate more cheese (parmesan) on top and drizzle with olive oil. Let cook until bubbles start to form. Transfer to oven under the broiler and with door open allow to brown (10-12 minutes). If you have whisked adequately the tortilla will rise. Take out and allow to cool for a few minutes.

Plating: Slice into adequate portions and plate, accompanied by a salad.

A tortilla is a versatile jack-of-all-trades. Differing from an omelette and simpler to make, you can chuck almost anything into it for a spectacular rich and filling starter or more. ***Buena suerte y buen provecho****!*

Notes

TORTILLA

TAPAS 101

The one Spanish class of dishes known the world

 STARTER  SPANISH  HOB  OVEN  FAST COOKING  30m SEAFOOD  PORK  MILD ★★ MODERATE

Description:

How long is a piece of string? There as many small tapas as they are hot dinners, to mix metaphors. Here are a few. They add up. Fast. Consider this class 101.

Ingredients

- Sourdough
- Small prawns (cooked or uncooked)
- Garlic (1 clove)
- Pimenton (smoked paprika)
- New Potatoes x8
- Manzanilla Olives (1 tin)
- Manchego
- Lime x 1
- Chorizo
- Cherry tomatoes (on vine)
- Red wine (glug)
- Jar of roasted peppers
- Olive oil
- Sea Salt and Pepper

Tools

- Knife
- Saucepan
- Ceramic gratinée dishes
- Ramekins
- Frying pan

Steps

Prep: These are essentially three different dishes- all easy. Preheat oven to **240°C**(464°F). Halve and boil new potatoes in salted water for 10 minutes. Drain in colander and let cool. Place in gratinée dish along with a tin of manzanilla olives and grated manchego on top. Drizzle with olive oil and lime and season. Maillard brown cubed chorizo (don't overdo) and put in gratinée with baby tomatoes on the vine and a glug of red wine. In third dish, put in prawns, crushed garlic clove, and 1 tblsp of paprika and olive oil. Slice and arrange manchego on a plate.

Cooking: Start the timer. Put potatoes in oven. At minute 5, the chorizo, at minute 15 the prawns. Toast bread. Remove all from oven at 23 minutes.

Plating: Serve on a wooden board, and let your diners pick and choose. Warn them that the food is screaming hot. Accompany with a cucumber and palmito salad, or a salad and a vinaigrette. (See CUCUMBER AND PALM HEARTS on page 268)

Tapas have almost become a cliché, but these tasty classics are a wonderful way to share food, and do not require a huge amount of prep (or cleaning!). This is a good way to pass your first course of Tapas 101.

Notes

TAPAS

GAMBAS

CHORIZO

PATATAS Y ACEITUNAS

PEPINO Y PALMITOS

MANCHEGO

LAMB KOFTA MEZZE

A lot of moving parts in a well-oiled machine

STARTER MIDDLE EAST HOB OVEN FAST COOKING 1hr LAMB VEGETABLE MILD ★★ MODERATE

Description:

Lamb kofta mezze is to street food what the Mona Lisa is to sketching. A mélange of dishes that constantly tickle the tastebuds. In isolation, starters. Together a whole meal.

Ingredients

- Minced lamb
- Aubergine x 1
- Garlic (1 clove)
- Spring Onions x 4
- Red chillies
- Jar of roasted red peppers
- Cucumber x 1
- Baby tomatoes x 8
- Tinned chickpeas
- Tahini (2 tblsp)
- Peperoncino paste (1 tblsp)
- Cumin Seeds
- Cardamom
- Cinnamon
- Coriander Leaves
- Cous cous
- Limes x 2
- Flatbread (either pita, piadini, or flatbread)
- Olive Oil
- Sea Salt and Pepper

Tools

- Knife
- Griddle pan
- Spice grinder
- Glass bowls & Ramekins

Steps

Prep: Preheat oven to **175°C**(350°F). ***Kofta:*** Toast and grind cumin and coriander seeds. Make a garlic paste from sea salt, ½ lime, and 1 clove garlic. Blend spices and garlic plus red peppers and spring onions in spice grinder (loosely, ***not*** to a liquid). Mix well into the lamb in a glass bowl with your hands. Season well. Make oblong patties and put bamboo skewers through them and put in fridge. ***Baba ganouche:*** Scorch aubergine evenly on hob until burnt. Then let cool, cut in half, and roast in oven for 35 minutes. Take out and let cool and scoop flesh into a glass bowl. Combine with 2 tblsp of tahini, sea salt and pepper, lime juice, peperoncino paste and olive oil. ***Couscous:*** Pour ¾ cup boiling water on 1 cup couscous and let sit for 3 minutes. Combine with diced cucumber, spring onion,halved baby tomatoes, chopped red peppers, olive oil, and lime. Season. ***Tzatziki:*** Blend Greek yoghurt, olive oil, diced cucumbers, cumin seeds, and sea salt and pepper. ***Hummus:*** In a spice grinder, combine chickpeas, tahini, lime, olive oil, chillies and marmite to a smooth consistency.

Cooking: Pat kofta dry, rub with olive oil, season liberally, then in a griddle pan, maillard brown, taking care they do not dry out. Griddle bread.

Plating: Plate kofta and couscous, ½ lime and triangles of bread. The rest let your diners dip. *No room for comment other than delish!*

LAMB KOFTA

COUS COUS | BABAGANOUSH | TZATZIKI | MARMITE HUMMUS

BUTTERNUT & SAGE RISOTTO

The joy of cooking vegetarian on a plate

STARTER

ITALIAN

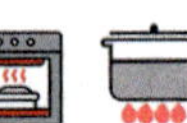
PREP

HOB

MEDIUM

1hr

VEGETABLE

NOT SPICY

EASY

Description:
The ideal dish for a kitchen supper, where the cook can talk while cooking, having assembled all the ingredients. Easy but precise.

Ingredients

- ◊ Arborio rice (250ml per person-1 cup)
- ◊ Butternut squash x 1
- ◊ Spring Onions
- ◊ Sage
- ◊ Peperoncino Paste (1 tsp)
- ◊ Chilli Flakes
- ◊ White wine
- ◊ Lime x 1
- ◊ Satsuma x 1
- ◊ Chicken or veggie boullion cube
- ◊ Parmesan
- ◊ Sea Salt and Black Pepper
- ◊ Olive Oil

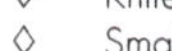

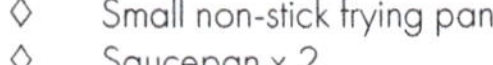

Tools

- ◊ Knife
- ◊ Small non-stick frying pan
- ◊ Saucepan x 2
- ◊ Spice grinder
- ◊ Spatula
- ◊ Glass bowl
- ◊ Probe digital thermometer
- ◊ Skimmer

Steps

Prep: Preheat oven to **175°C** (350°F). Cut butternut squash into cubes. Place on foil, drizzle with olive oil and sea salt, and roast in oven for 30 minutes until lightly Maillard browned. Remove and let cool. Take ½ of sage packet (remove stalks), and ½ of squash and blend with olive oil, salt, pepper, satsuma juice and chilli flakes until smooth. Grate parmesan.

Cooking: Make a ***brodo*** with water, lime juice, boullion cube, and white wine. Gently fry sage leaves until crispy for 2 minutes at 180°C (use probe thermometer) and drain on kitchen towel. Cook risotto (See MAKING RISOTTO on page 75). After 18 minutes, stir in puréed squash and blend throughly. At 21 minutes, parmesan cheese. At 22 minutes, the remainder of the squash cubes.

Plating: Slice into adequate portions and plate. Drizzle with olive oil and season. Place crispy sage on top.

An autumn evening kitchen light supper provides new possibilities, and is vegetarian to boot to suit you or your friends' desires.

Notes

BUTTERNUT & SAGE RISOTTO

GRATIN DAUPHINOIS

Cheesy potatoes- a classic accompanying dish-best supporting actor

STARTER

FRENCH

OVEN

MEDIUM

70m

VEGETABLE

MILD

EASY

Description:
The humble spud is elevated by the judicious application of a hint of garlic, cream, milk, cheese.and flavourings.

Ingredients

◇ Potato (Marist Piper or Red) x 2
◇ Garlic (1 clove)
◇ Cheddar
◇ Parmesan
◇ Milk
◇ Feta Cheese
◇ Rosemary
◇ Single cream (small)
◇ Dijon Mustard (1tblsp)
◇ Peperoncino paste (1 tsp)
◇ Chilli flakes
◇ Sea Salt and Black Pepper
◇ Olive Oil

Tools

◇ Knife
◇ Silicone Spoon
◇ Glass bowl
◇ Spice Grinder
◇ Large ceramic flan dish

Steps

Prep: Preheat oven to **175°C** (*350°F*). In the spice grinder, make a powder with rosemary leaves, sea salt and cracked pepper. Grate Parmesan and Cheddar and reserve. In a glass bowl, whisk single cream, dijon, chilli flakes and peperoncino. Peel and slice potatoes into thin slices. (Do this by slicing off a sliver lengthwise to enable the potato to lie flat and rocking back and forth with knife.) Alternatively, use a mandolin (wear a glove to keep injuries to a minimum). Pat dry on paper towels. In a large white ceramic gratin dish, rub a clove of garlic throughout and discard. Drizzle olive oil. Then arrange the potatoes in layers. On each layer season with sea salt and pepper, some of the rosemary spice, crumbled feta, and drizzled spiced cream. Repeat (probably two layers). Top with grated cheddar and parmesan. Pour a ½ cup (250mln) of milk evenly distributed on top.

Cooking: Cook for 50 minutes in oven. Check to make sure browned and not too dried out. If either, turn up heat to fan 180°C and/or add a splash of milk and cook for another 10-15 minutes. You want crisp edges.

Plating: If you are being cheffie, apportion in metal ring sizes as a side. Else, give a generous portion or be prepared to beat off your diners with a stick. This is very more-ish..

Simple, easy, and tasty. Okay, not a low calorie dish but a perfect autumn/winter antidote to dark, rainy evenings. As a leftover, a ready-made base to a tortilla or a soup.

Notes

GRATIN DAUPHINOIS

ONION TARTE TATIN

STARTER

FRENCH
OVEN

FRYING

MEDIUM

7om

VEGETABLE

MILD
EASY

Caramelised onions with salty ham and cheese on a crisp puff pastry

Description:

This twist on a classic French fruit pastry has many different tastes: sweet, umami, caramelisation, and salt from the addition of wafer thin Parma ham and English cheddar.

Ingredients

- ◇ Red Onions x 4
- ◇ Puff pastry
- ◇ Cheddar
- ◇ Parma Ham (1 packet)
- ◇ Garlic (1 clove)
- ◇ Brown rice vinegar (1 tsp)
- ◇ Ponzu (1 tsp)
- ◇ Sake (1 tsp)
- ◇ Mirin (1 tsp)
- ◇ Brown Sugar (1 tsp)
- ◇ English Mustard (1 tsp)
- ◇ Sea Salt and Black Pepper

Tools

- ◇ Knife
- ◇ Apple Corer
- ◇ Spatula
- ◇ Spice Grinder
- ◇ Small Frying pan
- ◇ Cartouche

Steps

Prep: Preheat oven to **175°C** (*350°F*). In a pestle & mortar, crush the garlic, sea salt, and rice vinegar into a paste. In the spice grinder, blend the paste, ponzu, sake, mirin, mustard and brown sugar. Halve the onions and top and tail them. Then either pop the middle out or using an apple corer.

Cooking: In the small frying pan, add a drizzle of olive oil. Lay the onion halves cut side down. Add a small amount of water and on a low heat cook for 15-20 minutes covered with a ***cartouche***. (See MAKING A CARTOUCHE on page 76) Meanwhile on a floured surface roll out the chilled puff pastry and cut a circle slightly large than the diameter of the frying pan. Add the sauce to the pan. The heat should be medium/high, but not too much that onions burn but enough that the sauce thickens. Carefully turn the onions over, so the cut side is up. Take off the heat and let cool (5 minutes). With the apple corer, cut plugs of cheddar cheese. Put these in the center of the onions (see picture). Then arrange wafer thin parma ham on top. Cover with the puff pastry circle, tuck in the edges, and prick all over with a fork to allow the steam to escape. Put in oven (on high shelf) for 35-40 minutes, checking to see pastry is not burning.

Plating: Take frying pan from oven USING OVEN GLOVES and allow to cool (5 minutes). Put an upturned plate on top, and flip in one smooth motion. Voilà. A tarte tatin!. If you want the onions to char a bit put under the broiler for a minute or two, but keep an eye out! AND ALWAYS USE OVEN GLOVES. But I repeat myself. Accompany with a salad. If a main course or a few leaves on the side as a starter. *This simple dish produces complex tastes which are a sheer joy to eat.*

Notes

ONION TARTE TATIN
PARMA HAM | CHEESE

WHITETIGER
FOOD DREAMS

MAINS

SCALLOP & SHRIMP QUICHE

A light quiche with succulent scallops and a tang of spicy

 MAIN  BRITISH  OVEN  MEDIUM COOKING  45m  SEAFOOD  MILD EASY

Description:
Cream, eggs, fluffy whipped egg whites, scallops and shrimp in a sumptuous flaky pastry crust

Ingredients

- ◊ Puff Pastry (store bought)
- ◊ Eggs x 4
- ◊ Single Cream
- ◊ Dijon Mustard
- ◊ Shrimp (pre-cooked)
- ◊ Scallops
- ◊ Cheddar
- ◊ Spring Onions x 3
- ◊ Parmesan
- ◊ Parsley
- ◊ Old Bay
- ◊ Frank's Hot Sauce

Tools

- ◊ Pie Pan (glass, ceramic or metal)
- ◊ Glass Bowls x 2
- ◊ Ceramic Baking Beans
- ◊ Hand Mixer
- ◊ Silicone Brush

Steps

Prep: Preheat oven to **210C** (425°F). Roll out pastry to thin layer and trace outside the pie dish to leave enough room for the sides. Crimp the edges with your thumbs and chill. Separate yolks and whites and put in two glass bowls. In the yolk bowl, combine single cream, grated cheeses, mustard, a dash of Frank's Hot Sauce,sea salt, and pepper. Whip the egg whites until peaked with a hand mixer.

Cooking: Blind bake the crust for 15-20 minutes. (See CRISP PASTRY on page 67). When you check, make sure the bottom is browned or else remove the foil and baking beans and brown up for a few minutes. Once browned, paint the base with olive oil using the silicone brush. Sauté the shrimps in olive oil for 2 minutes with Old Bay seasoning. Add spring onions for 2 minutes. Let cool. Combine egg whites and yolk/cream mixture by carefully folding in the peaked whites. Add the shrimps and onions to the cream/yolk mixture and pour into the crust. Place the raw scallops arranged on top of the mixture with a dash of Frank's on each one. Grate more cheese on top and lightly season. Bake at **175°C** for 35-40 minutes.

Plating: Serve on plate and drizzle with olive oil accompanied by a salad.

A light but rich supper to remind you of a seaside walk on a beach in the salt air.

 *Notes*

SCALLOP & SHRIMP QUICHE
JUS-ROL
JUS-ROL
ESSENTIAL WAITROSE
SINGLE CREAM

SHORT RIB RAGU

A sumptuous slow-cooked tomato sauce with short ribs

MAIN

ITALIAN
HOB

OVEN

BRAISING

3hrs

BEEF

MILD

EASY

Description:
The gift which keeps on giving. Slow, easy, rich, smoky. Better even a few days later.

Ingredients

- ◊ Short ribs (250g per person)
- ◊ Variety of Tomatoes
- ◊ Sofritto (Onions, Celery, Carrot)
- ◊ Red Onion
- ◊ White Onion
- ◊ Garlic (1 clove crushed to paste))
- ◊ Lime
- ◊ Flour
- ◊ Tomato Paste(1 tblsp)
- ◊ Sweet Smoked Paprika
- ◊ Worcestershire Sauce
- ◊ Peperoncino paste
- ◊ Red Wine
- ◊ Olive Oil
- ◊ Sea Salt and Pepper
- ◊ Parmesan
- ◊ Flat Leaf Parsley
- ◊ Tagliatelle or Pappardelle

Tools

- ◊ Covered Casserole
- ◊ Frying Pan
- ◊ Knife

Steps

Prep: Preheat oven to **140°C** (284°F) Pat ribs dry. Place in plastic bag along with flour, smoked paprika, sea salt and pepper and shake to coat. Prep sofritto into fairly large chunks and set in glass bowl.

Cooking: In casserole on high heat on hob, Maillard brown the ribs on all sides and remove to another glass bowl. (See BRAISING on page 132) Add ***sofritto*** and more olive oil to pan, then add tomatoes, lime zest, juice of 1/2 lime, Worcestershire sauce, tomato paste, and seasoning and de-glaze with red wine (500ml). Turn heat down for several minutes. Place browned ribs on top. Cover with foil and lid and cook in oven for 2 hours. After two hours, remove bone and any gristle and shred or chop the meat and add back to sauce. Return to the oven for another 1 hour. Boil pasta in salted water (8-10 minutes or as per packet), drain, and drizzle olive oil.

Plating: Serve in pasta bowl, top with parsley and grated parmesan and drizzle with olive oil accompanied by a salad.

The depth of flavour and richness of this dish is sublime. As a follow-up lunch on toast with cheddar slice and baby spinach.... legendary.

Notes

SHORT RIB RAGU

GAMBAS OLD BAY

A mixture of cuisines and spices. Gotta be fusion.

MAIN FUSION OVEN FAST COOKING 20m SEAFOOD MILD EASY

Description:

Old Bay prawns. A nod to the Spanish but with Chesapeake Bay spices, hummus, and palmitos (hearts of palm), an Argentine friend's favourite legume. You tell me.

Ingredients

- Large prawns (shells on min.4 per person)
- Old Bay Spice
- Lime x 2
- Garbanzo beans
- Tahini (1 ½ tblsp)
- Franks Hot sauce (1 tsp)
- Liquid smoke (1 tsp)
- Hearts of Palm
- Lamb's Lettuce

Sauce rose

- Ketchup (1 tblsp)
- Mayonnaise (1 tblsp)
- Greek Yoghurt (1 tblsp)
- Peperoncino paste (1 tsp)
- Olive oil
- Sea Salt and Pepper
- Rustic pain or ciabatta rolls

Tools

- Knife
- Ceramic gratinée dishes
- Glass Bowls
- Ramekins
- Blender

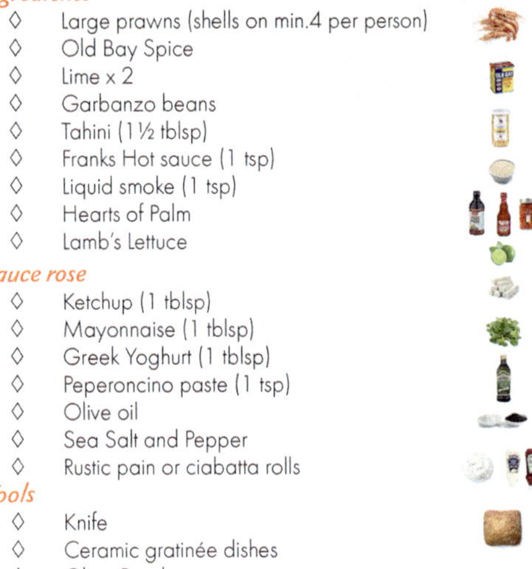

Steps

Prep: Preheat oven to **240°C**(464°F). Slice palm hearts. Toss prawns in Glass bowls with Old Bay, Sea salt, black pepper, juice of lime, and olive oil. Mix well to make sure they are fully coated. In blender, blitz tin of garbanzo beans, tahini, lime juice, Frank's Hot Sauce, sea salt, pepper, and olive oil until smooth, adding olive oil gradually until the consistency is smooth and creamy. Make sauce rose. (See MAKING A CREAMY SALAD DRESSING on page 130)

Cooking: Place prawns in ceramic gratinée dishes and cook for 10-12 minutes until sizzling. With 3 minutes to go, put rustic rolls in oven on bottom shelf. .

Plating: Serve in the gratinée dishes along with the palmito salad, sauce rose and hummus. Provide finger dipping bowls for the aftermath, and let guests mop up various juices as they see fit.

A light supper for a summer evening, or perhaps a winter one. Doesn't matter.

Notes

GAMBAS OLD BAY

PALMITOS|SMOKED HUMMUS|SAUCE ROSE

BLITZED POUSSIN

Young chickens wise beyond their years

MAIN

BRITISH

MICROWAVE

HOB

OVEN

FAST COOKING

45m

POULTRY

MILD

★★ MODERATE

Description:

A simple dish meriting inclusion in any brasserie or gastropub menu. Crispy. Moist. Succulent. Blitzed refers to the high temperature blasting in the oven.

Ingredients

- Poussin x 1
- Large Potato x 1
- Purple Spring Onions
- Frozen Baby Spinach
- Lime
- Jalapeño Sauce
- Olive Oil
- Salt & Pepper
- Chilli Flakes
- Splash of white wine
- Vegetable oil (for frying)
- Tools
- Skillet
- Gratinée Dish
- Glass Bowl
- Poultry Shears
- Strainer
- Masher (for spinach)
- Silicone brush
- Julienne peeler

Steps

Prep: Preheat oven to **240°C** (464°F). Using poultry shears, cut on either side of backbone of poussin and splay out. Then cut down the middle of the breastbone to split into two parts. Season both sides with sea salt and crushed pepper. ***Shoestring fries:*** Peel and julienne the potato into matchsticks using the julienne peeler. Wash the matchsticks in cold water. Then squeeze the water out of them with paper towel and spread them out on more paper towel to dry them out. Trim and halve spring onions and place in gratinée dish with some olive oil.

Cooking: In hot skillet with a film of olive oil, Maillard brown both sides of poussin. When browned, place skin side up in gratinée dish. Squeeze one lime, add a splash of white wine, and paint on jalapeño sauce. Season again and sprinkle some chilli flakes.. Set your stopwatch. Bake at **240°C** for **23 minutes**. At 13 min check colour and baste. NOTE: THIS IS HOT OVEN, SO PAY ATTENTION. Meanwhile, heat vegetable oil to **190°C (375°F)** in pan and in batches fry the potatoes for 3-5 minutes until golden, removing them to drain on yet more paper towel. In a glass bowl, put frozen baby spinach cubes and cook in microwave for 5 minutes. Take out and squeeze all the water out in the sink with a potato masher. Season, add ½ lime, and olive oil. Blend into leaves and return to microwave for 2 minutes right before serving. Remove screaming-hot blitzed poussin from oven.

Plating: Drizzle olive oil on poussin and serve with some dijon mustard on side. *Straight to the point. No frills. Hot from the oven, the skin is crisp and the juiciness goes down to the bone. Don't overcook!*

BLITZED POUSSIN
SHOESTRING FRIES | SPINACH

JAPANESE GINGER PORK

Buta No Shōgayaki (Japanese Ginger Pork)

MAIN

JAPANESE

GRIDDLE

FAST COOKING

1.1hr

PORK

MILD

★
EASY

Description:

A variation on a classic Japanese recipe (adding chillies and coriander). The cornstarch velvets and tenderises the meat, also adding body to the sauce. The dark soy and sugar augment the Maillard browning for a rich dark brown colour.

Ingredients

- ◊ Pork Steaks
- ◊ Spring Onions
- ◊ Red Chillies
- ◊ Coriander

Marinade

- ◊ Garlic (1 clove)
- ◊ Ginger (1 knob)
- ◊ Dark Soy Sauce (1 tblsp)
- ◊ Cornstarch (1.5 tblsp)
- ◊ Mirin (1 tblsp)
- ◊ Sake (1 tblsp)
- ◊ Ponzu (1 tsp)
- ◊ Sea Salt and Black Pepper
- ◊ Dark sugar (1 tsp)
- ◊ Olive Oil

Tools

- ◊ Glass Bowl
- ◊ Griddle Pan
- ◊ Spice Grinder
- ◊ Pestle & Mortar
- ◊ Chef's Knife

Steps

Prep: Slice Pork steaks ***cross grain*** into thin strips. Crush garlic and ginger in pestle with sea salt and olive oil into paste. In spice grinder blend all marinade ingredients (including paste). Pour over pork strips and refrigerate. Just before cooking, slice chillies and spring onions diagonally.

Cooking: Heat griddle pan to screaming hot with a drizzle of olive oil. Take out strips and dry on paper towel. Stir fry pork in small batches until Maillard Brown. Take out browned meat and put in bowl. Just before serving, add more oil to pan and fry chillies and spring onions 1-2 minutes. Put in marinade and let thicken (add sake if necessary). You want some thick liquid. Season carefully to taste.

Serving/Plating: Top with coriander and added chillies if desired. Serve on sizzling griddle pan on wooden board with tongs. Accompany with rice and a salad. (See COOKING RICE on page 74)

In addition to being a wonderful combination of taste sensations, this is an impressive dish sure to wow your diners.

Notes

豚の生姜焼き
BUTA NO SHŌGAYAKI
Ginger Pork

SEA BREAM WITH LENTILS

Light and filling crispy whitefish with a lentil salad

MAIN | BRITISH | HOB | FAST COOKING | 30m | SEAFOOD | NOT SPICY | EASY

Description:

Crisp skin-on pan fried sea bream with a tangy salad of lentils, olives, feta, carrots, and spring onions and mixed tomatoes, lime, and parsley salad.

Ingredients

- ◊ Sea Bream fillets x2
- ◊ Puy lentils
- ◊ Feta Cheese
- ◊ Manzanilla Olives (***Fragata***)
- ◊ Carrot x1
- ◊ Baby tomatoes
- ◊ Flat leaf parsley
- ◊ Lime
- ◊ Olive Oil
- ◊ Sea Salt and Black Pepper

Dressing

- ◊ Oil & Vinegar Vinaigrette
- ◊ Frying pans x 2
- ◊ Glass Bowls x 2
- ◊ Chef's Knife
- ◊ Spatula
- ◊ Peeler

Steps

Prep: If necessary, cook lentils. Otherwise buy the pre-cooked. Finely peel and chop carrots, olives and spring onions and fry gently for 4-5 minutes just to take the edge off. Mix in bowl along with feta and chopped parsley. Make a vinaigrette (See MAKING A SALAD DRESSING on page 69) and dress the lentils. Halve tomatoes and put in separate bowl with chopped parsley and drizzle with juice of ½ lime and olive oil and seasoning just before serving. Pat dry the sea bream fillets on both sides. Rub olive oil into the skin side and season well with sea salt and cracked black pepper.

Cooking: Heat a frying pan on medium heat and place bream skin side down. Cook for 4 minutes. Carefully turn with a sharp spatula (the skin is delicate). It should be golden brown. Cook on the other side for 2 minutes.

Serving/Plating: Arrange both salads on plate using circular moulds. Place fillet, a lime wedge and drizzle with olive oil.

The simplest things are sometimes the best, but rely on split-second timing.

Notes

Denby

CHICKEN & MUSHROOM PIE

Robust chicken and forest mushroom pie

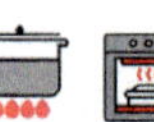

MAIN | BRITISH | HOB | OVEN | MEDIUM COOKING | 1hr20m | POULTRY | MILD | EASY

Description:

This one pan dish is the gift which keeps on giving. A rich, spicy, umami cheese sauce provides the base for a substantial evening meal which can carry on into leftovers the next day.

Ingredients

- Chicken breast (pre-cooked)
- Forest, exotic, or any mixed mushrooms
- Carrot
- Spring Onions
- Olives stuffed with Pimentos
- Celery
- Ponzu (1 tblsp)
- Vermouth or white wine (Glug)

Cheese Sauce

- Cheddar Cheese
- Parmesan Cheese
- Flour
- Milk
- English Mustard (1 tblsp)
- Peperoncino Paste (1 tblsp)
- Sea Salt and Black Pepper
- Puff Pastry
- Egg x 1

Tools

- Frying Pan
- Roasting tin
- Knife
- Glass bowl
- Silicone brush

Steps

Prep: Preheat oven to **175°C** (350°F). Cut all ingredients into decent sized uniform chunks.

Cooking: In hot deep frying pan, sauté mushrooms first until browned (4-5 minutes) and then add all the other ingredients (adding Ponzu and white wine or vermouth at end) and turn heat down to medium (5 minutes). Transfer to white roasting tin. In saucepan, make a cheese sauce adding the mustard and chilli paste (See MAKING A ROUX on page 71). Mix all in roasting tin. Roll out puff pastry into an oblong shape. Paint edges of tin with egg wash, place pastry on top and cut with scissors to leave a one inch excess. Crimp and stick to edge of pan with thumbs and then a fork. Paint egg wash on pastry and grate parmesan on top. Season. Put in oven at **175°C** (350°F) for **40-45 minutes**.

Plating: Nothing fancy. Accompany with a salad.

What is not to like? A dish which ticks all the boxes.

Notes

CHICKEN | FOREST MUSHROOMS
ONE PAN PIE

BABY BACK RIBS

MAIN AMERICAN HOB OVEN SLOW COOKING 3hrs PORK MILD EASY

Fall off the bone stuff. Deep and smoky

Description:

No need for a barbeque with this dish, though you can easily imagine it. Something to make when you have an afternoon to kill and a nap to take.

Ingredients

- Baby back ribs (Rack x 1 per person)
- Banana Shallots
- Sweetcorn cobs x 2
- Tamed jalapeño peppers
- Pointy cabbage
- Liquid smoke
- BBQ sauce
- Frank's Hot Sauce
- Lime
- Ponzu
- Satsuma or Tangerine
- Mixed baby tomatoes
- Coriander

For the Dry rub (spices roasted and ground)

- Cumin
- Coriander Seeds
- Fennel seeds
- Celery Salt
- Sea Salt
- Black Pepper

Tools

- Roasting tin
- Glass Bowls
- Basting brush
- Knife

Steps

Prep: Preheat oven to **210°C** (410°F) Pat ribs dry. Slice banana shallots lengthways and place in bottom of roasting tin (after a drizzle of olive oil). Roast spices, in small pan over hob for a minute or so and grind in the spice grinder with sea salt and pepper. Using plastic gloves, massage into all part of the ribs and arrange them on top of the shallots, fat side up. Drizzle juice of one lime and one satsuma, and glugs of Frank's Hot Sauce and liquid smoke (but NO BBQ sauce yet). Meanwhile, cut kernels off the corn cobs, and blanch in boiling salted water for 2 minutes. Drain under cold water. Halve tomatoes and jalapeños and mix in glass bowl. Drizzle with lime and olive oil. Scatter coriander and season. Make ponzu sauce. (See MAKING A CREAMY SALAD DRESSING on page 70) Discard the outer leaves of the pointy cabbage, then shred by cutting. Mix sauce and shredded cabbage, cover with cling film, and put in fridge. ***Cooking:*** Put ribs in oven for 15-20 minutes until they are browned slightly, then remove. Apply BBQ sauce with a silicon brush evenly. Turn oven temp down to **140°C** (284°F). Cover with foil and bake for 2.5 hrs. Take out and remove foil. Season. Baste again with more BBQ sauce and put underneath a hot **240°C** (446°F) broiler for five minutes until the fat sizzles and the ribs colour.

Plating: Plate up with the ribs, corn salsa, ponzu slaw and shallots. *A sight for sore eyes and sticky fingers.*

BABY BACK RIBS
CORN SALSA | PONZU SLAW

AUBERGINE PARMEGIANA

A quick vegetarian delight in a gratinée dish

 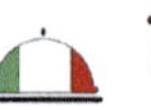     

MAIN | ITALIAN | HOB | OVEN | FAST COOKING | 40m | VEGETABLE | MILD | EASY

Description:
Individual servings of an Italian classic cooked at high heat in an oven with griddled aubergine for a smoky taste with four types of cheese.

Ingredients

- ◊ Aubergines x 2

Tomato sauce

- ◊ Spring Onions
- ◊ Tomatoes
- ◊ Tomato paste (1tblsp)
- ◊ Red Wine Vinegar (1tsp)
- ◊ Guindilla Peppers
- ◊ Peperoncino Paste (1tsp)
- ◊ Oregano (fresh or dried- 1tsp)

- ◊ Cottage Cheese
- ◊ Mozzarella
- ◊ Greek Yoghurt
- ◊ Parmesan
- ◊ Chicory
- ◊ Roquefort or Danish Blue Cheese

Salad Dressing

- ◊ Lime
- ◊ Olive Oil
- ◊ Sea Salt and Pepper

Tools

- ◊ Gratinée Dish
- ◊ Griddle Pan
- ◊ Deep Covered Frying Pan (for tomato sauce)
- ◊ Glass Bowl
- ◊ Knife

Steps

Prep: Preheat oven to **240°C (464°F).** Slice aubergines horizontally to 1.5cm thickness. Season them and drizzle olive oil. In a high heat griddle pan, fry until griddle marks are prominent on both sides (3-4 mins/side). Reserve in glass bowl. Chop spring onions and tomatoes, and in a deep saucepan, make the tomato sauce, including the guindilla peppers and peperoncino paste. Let simmer 20 min.

Cooking: Place alternate layers of aubergines and tomato sauce, dotting dollops of cottage cheese, mozzarella, and Greek yoghurt on each layer before starting another. Top with grated parmesan and drizzle with olive oil. Bake in oven for 23 minutes. Let cool for 3 minutes before serving in the gratinée dish, for this will be piping hot.

Plating: Serve in gratinée dish. Arrange chicory leaves with crumbled Roquefort or blue cheese, accompanied by a lime salad dressing.(See MAKING A SALAD DRESSING on page 69)

*Straightforward. Rich. Punches over its weight. Perfect to inspire your diners to **fare la scarpetta** (lick the dish!).*

Notes

AUBERGINE PARMEGIANA

CHICORY & ROQUEFORT

ROAST COD AND CHORIZO

The perfect marriage of fish and pork

 MAIN
 SPANISH
 HOB
 OVEN
 FAST COOKING
 45m
 SEAFOOD
 MILD
 EASY

Description:
The iconic taste of chorizo and tomato joins together with crisp and flaky roast cod

Ingredients

- ◊ Cod fillets x 2

Tomato sauce

- ◊ Chorizo
- ◊ Tomatoes x 4
- ◊ White beans (*judion or cannelini*)
- ◊ Spring Onions
- ◊ Tomato paste
- ◊ Sweet smoked paprika
- ◊ Guindilla peppers (***Fragata*** or ***Perella***)
- ◊ Red wine (250ml)
- ◊ Spring onions
- ◊ Sea salt and Black Pepper
- ◊ Sourdough Toast
- ◊ Manchego

Tools

- ◊ Gratinée dish
- ◊ Deep Frying Pan with lid

Steps

Prep: Preheat oven to **240°C** (464°F). Chop chorizo into bite-sized pieces, then slice the tomatoes, spring onions, and guindillas.
Cooking: Maillard brown the chorizo until well-browned and the fat rendered (5-7 minutes). Add spring onions and guindillas and fry gently for 2 minutes. Add rest of sauce ingredients, cover and simmer to the side for 30 minutes. Pat dry the cod fillets, season liberally and rub olive oil on both sides. In hot frying pan, cook one side for 3 minutes until browned, then 1 minute on the other side. In a gratinée dish, ladle the chorizo bean sauce, and gently place the cod fillet with the browned side up. Cook in hot oven for 8-10 minutes. Toast slices of sourdough.
Plating: Serve on plate and drizzle olive oil. Accompany with sourdough toast and cheese on the side and possibly a salad.

Cod can be bland. Not so with the smoky sour garlicky taste of chorizo and the robustness of the white beans.

Notes

ROAST COD ON CHORIZO AND BEANS

SZECHUAN CUMIN LAMB

Lamb and Cumin and Chilli-a match made in heaven

MAIN | CHINESE | WOK | FAST COOKING-WOK | 1hr | LAMB | V. SPICY | EASY

Description:

In many cuisines, lamb and cumin are often partners. No more so than in this Szechuan classic dish. Can be on either flat noodles or rice.

Ingredients

- Lamb Steaks
- Spring Onions
- Bak Choi
- Red Chillies x 2 or 3
- Coriander

Marinade

- Garlic (1 clove)
- Ginger (1 knob)
- Dark Soy Sauce (1 tblsp)
- Cornstarch (1.5 tblsp)
- Shaoxing Wine (1 tblsp)
- Sea Salt and Black Pepper
- Dark sugar (1 tsp)
- Olive Oil

Tools

- Glass Bowl
- Wok
- Spice Grinder
- Pestle & Mortar
- Chef's Knife

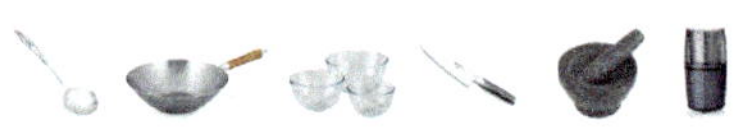

Steps

Prep: Slice Lamb steaks ***cross grain*** into thin strips. Crush garlic and ginger in pestle & mortar with sea salt and olive oil into paste. In spice grinder blend all marinade ingredients (including paste). Pour over lamb strips and refrigerate for minimum 1 hour. Just before cooking, slice chillies and spring onions diagonally, bak choi horizontally

Cooking: (See FAST COOKING-WOK on page 83) Heat wok to smoking hot with a drizzle of olive oil. Take out strips and dry on paper towel. Stir fry lamb in small batches until Maillard Brown. Take out browned meat and put in bowl. Just before serving, add more oil to wok and fry chillies, spring onions and bak choi for 1-2 minutes. Return meat to wok. Put in marinade and let thicken (add wine if necessary). You want some thick liquid. Season carefully to taste.

Serving/Plating: Top with coriander and added chillies if desired. Serve on sizzling wok on wooden board with tongs. Accompany with rice. (See COOKING RICE on page 74)

As this dish is Szechuan, don't be shy with the chillies. Who dares wins.

Notes

SZECHUAN CUMIN LAMB

HONEY GINGER DUCK BREAST

MAIN BRITISH HOB/OVEN FAST COOKING 20m FOWL NOT SPICY EASY

Quick supper/salad which is tart and sweet and savoury

Description:

Duck breast has to be done right. Tough to get crispy skin, rendered fat, medium rare, and taste. This light supper does it with an apple/celeriac remoulade.

Ingredients

◊ Duck Breasts x 2

Marinade

◊ Ginger
◊ Soy
◊ Mirin
◊ Honey
◊ Garlic (1 clove)
◊ Apple
◊ Carrot
◊ Celeriac
◊ Flat Leaf Parsley

Ponzu Dressing

◊ Mayonnaise (dollop)
◊ Greek Yoghurt (dollop)
◊ Rice Vinegar (capful)
◊ Dijon Mustard (1 tsp)
◊ Yuzu
◊ Ponzu (1tblsp)
◊ Light Soy Sauce (1tsp)
◊ Sea Salt and Black Pepper
◊ Olive Oil

Tools

◊ Knife
◊ Glass Bowl
◊ Frying pan
◊ White roasting tin
◊ Tongs

Steps

Prep: Preheat oven to **220°C** (405°F). Peel and julienne the apple, carrot, and celeriac. Make a ponzu dressing. (See MAKING A CREAMY SALAD DRESSING on page 70). Combine all in a glass bowl and mix thoroughly. Crush a clove of garlic, and dice the ginger before whizzing all (including mirin, honey and soy sauce) in the spice grinder. Adjust the consistency with some olive oil. It wants to be thick and not runny. Pat dry the duck breasts. Score the fat in a criss cross pattern. Season well.

Cooking: Place duck breasts in a ***dry cold*** frying pan skin side down. Turn on hob to medium high and allow duck fat to render and become crisp (5-6 minutes). Turn for 1 minute. Place in a roasting tin skin side up in oven to roast for 7-9 minutes and cover with sauce. Remove and allow to rest (5 minutes)

Assembly/Plating: Slice duck thinly at an angle and plate along with the remoulade. Accompany with sourdough toast if desired.

A veritable greatest hits of umami, sweet and tartness with the rich duck.

Notes

HONEY GINGER DUCK BREAST

YUZU CELERIAC & APPLE REMOULADE

OSSO BUCO

Slow and easy veal shanks.

MAIN

ITALIAN

HOB
OVEN

SLOW COOKING
1.5hrs

VEGETABLE

MILD

EASY

Description:

Meltingly soft and tasty with an added hit of bone marrow, parmesan, and citrus. Hits all the right notes, and a one-pot wonder to boot.

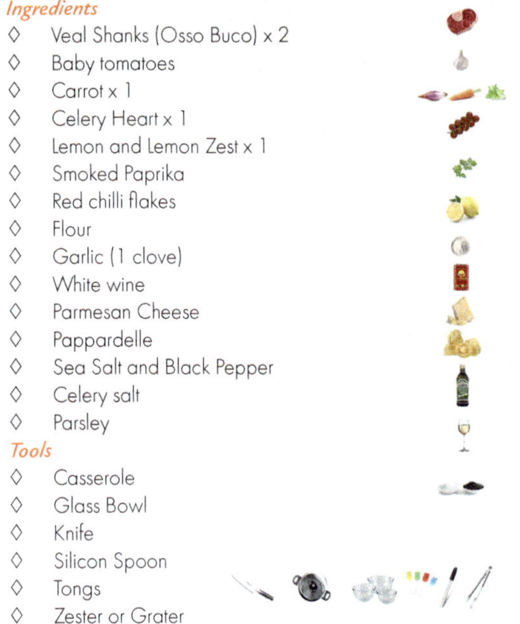

Ingredients

- Veal Shanks (Osso Buco) x 2
- Baby tomatoes
- Carrot x 1
- Celery Heart x 1
- Lemon and Lemon Zest x 1
- Smoked Paprika
- Red chilli flakes
- Flour
- Garlic (1 clove)
- White wine
- Parmesan Cheese
- Pappardelle
- Sea Salt and Black Pepper
- Celery salt
- Parsley

Tools

- Casserole
- Glass Bowl
- Knife
- Silicon Spoon
- Tongs
- Zester or Grater

Steps

Prep: Preheat oven to **140°C** (284°F). Dice ***mirepoix*** or ***sofritto*** of carrots, celery, and onions. Zest a lemon and reserve. Crush garlic, sea salt, and juice of 1/2 the lemon in pestle and mortar to a paste. In a plastic bag, put flour, sea salt, pepper, and smoked paprika and shake well. Put in each shank and shake the bag to coat evenly.

Cooking: On high heat on the hob, Maillard brown each side of the flank and reserve to glass bowl. Drizzle olive oil in the pot and put in the mirepoix to sweat, stirring constantly. Add the garlic paste. Return the osso buco to the casserole, put in whole baby tomatoes, add a good glug of white wine, drizzle with more oil, cover tightly with foil and cover, and put in oven for 2 hours. Take from oven and scatter a lot of grated parmesan and chilli flakes on top. Boil the pappardelle in salted water (fresh 2-3 minutes, dried 8-10 minutes). Turn the oven to broil (hot) and broil the osso buco until the cheese is a deep golden Maillard brown.

Plating: Drain pappardelle and drizzle with olive oil. Serve the osso buco and surround with the vegetables. Scatter parsley on top. Accompany with a salad and a vinaigrette (one with celery salt is a nice option).(See MAKING A SALAD DRESSING on page 69)

The meat is soft, the sauce tangy on the papardelle, but the star of the show is sucking the bone marrow and crisp parmesan out of the centre bone at the end. Mmmm.....

Notes

OSSO BUCO | PAPPARDELLE

PANCETTA E CARCIOFI RAVIOLI

Lardons and artichoke parmesan ravioli.

 MAIN  ITALIAN HOB  FAST COOKING  20min  PORK  MILD  EASY

Description:

The sauce turns this quick dish into a painting of the sun. Rich. Sublime. Simple.

Ingredients

- ◊ Ravioli stuffed with Parmigiana and Ricotta
- ◊ Smoked lardons
- ◊ Artichoke Hearts (***Giu Giu*** is the best)
- ◊ Orange and red baby tomatoes x 6
- ◊ Sour Cream (small)
- ◊ Parmesan (½ cup)
- ◊ Peperoncino Paste (again ***Giu Giu***)
- ◊ Chilli flakes
- ◊ Guindilla peppers (***Fragata***)
- ◊ White wine (glug)
- ◊ Olive oil
- ◊ Sea Salt and Black Pepper

Tools

- ◊ Deep Frying Pan
- ◊ Saucepan
- ◊ Colander
- ◊ Knife
- ◊ Silicon Spoon
- ◊ Tongs
- ◊ Spice Grinder

Steps

Prep: Wash and spin lettuce. Chop guindilla peppers and halve tomatoes and artichoke hearts. Make the sauce using 4-5 baby tomatoes, sour cream, peperoncino paste, chilli flakes, grated parmesan, olive oil, sea salt and pepper, and red wine vinegar. Blitz fresh ingredients in spice grinder until smooth. The colour should be orangish. Boil salted water for pasta.

Cooking: On high heat on the hob in deep pan brown lardons, artichoke hearts and guindilla peppers. Drain oil. When you put the ravioli on to boil (4 minutes) mix the sauce into the lardons/artichokes/peppers, stirring constantly over low heat. Blend in a glug of white wine. When the pasta is cooked, drain in colander, return to the deep pan and toss all the ingredients.

Plating: Plate the ravioli in a pasta bowl. Scatter parsley and drizzle olive oil on top. Accompany with a salad and a vinaigrette.(See MAKING A SALAD DRESSING on page 130)

A very quick (20 minutes max) light supper which has you wishing it would never end.

Notes

PANCETTA E CARCIOFI RAVIOLI

TAGLIATELLE LARDONS BAK CHOI

Lardons, bak choi, and griddled white asparagus

MAIN FUSION HOB GRIDDLE FAST COOKING 20min PORK NOT SPICY EASY

Description:
A thick rasher of lardons and fresh white asparagus survived a journey from Paris to create a quick memorable supper to be repeated.

Ingredients

- ◊ Fresh tagliatelle
- ◊ Lardons (if possible made from a rasher)
- ◊ White asparagus (thick)
- ◊ Spring onions
- ◊ Soured Cream
- ◊ Parmesan
- ◊ White wine (glug)
- ◊ Lime
- ◊ Olive oil
- ◊ Sea Salt and Black Pepper

Tools

- ◊ Deep Frying Pan
- ◊ Saucepan
- ◊ Griddle pan
- ◊ Knife
- ◊ Silicon spoon

Steps

Prep: Boil salted water for pasta. Cube lardons from rasher if bought. Halve asparagus spears lengthwise. Slice spring onions and bak choi. Grate parmesan.

Cooking: On high heat on the hob in deep frying pan Maillard brown lardons. Drain oil. Sauté spring onions for 1 minute. When you put the tagliatelle on to boil (4 minutes) , sauté asparagus spears in screaming hot griddle pan. Then add the sour cream and parmesan to the deep pan, stirring constantly over low heat. Blend in a glug of white wine. When the pasta is cooked, drain in colander, return to the deep pan and toss all the ingredients, adding the bak choi at the last minute.

Plating: Plate the tagliatelle in a pasta bowl. Season with sea salt and black pepper. Scatter parsley and drizzle olive oil on top. Arrange asparagus to the side, season, and drizzle ½ lime and olive oil. Accompany with a salad and a vinaigrette.(See MAKING A SALAD DRESSING on page 130)

This impromptu dish had such pleasant memories that it deserved a place and should be repeated the minute you see ingredients like fresh asparagus (white or green) in a market. Try to use the thick rasher and make your own lardons but ready made smoked lardons will work fine.

Notes

AGLIATELLE LARDONS BAK CHOI
WHITE ASPARAGUS

GOCHUJANG PORK BELLY

A slightly tamed version of the fiery Korean dish

MAIN | KOREAN | WOK | FAST COOKING-WOK | 30m | PORK | X. SPICY | EASY

Description:

The fiery pepper paste ***gochujang*** *is the background of this tasty Korean-style dish. I have ratcheted back on the amount of garlic.*

Ingredients

- Pork Belly Slices
- Red Onion x 2
- Spring Onions x 4
- Pointy Cabbage x 1
- Gochujang paste (2 tblsp)
- Red Chillies x 2 or 3
- Green Chillies x 1
- Coriander
- Basmati Rice
- Seasoned Crispy Seaweed
- Kimchi (store-bought)

Marinade

- Garlic (2 cloves)
- Ginger (1 knob)
- Dark Soy Sauce (1 tblsp)
- Honey (1 tblsp)
- Toasted sesame oil (1 tsp)
- Sea Salt and Black Pepper
- Olive Oil

Tools

- Glass Bowl
- Wok
- Spice Grinder
- Pestle & Mortar
- Chef's Knife

Steps

Prep: If you haven't bought the frozen pork belly slices in a Korean store (and let them defrost), take raw pork belly, remove the rind, freeze, and slice thinly. Crush garlic and ginger in pestle & mortar with sea salt and olive oil into paste. In spice grinder blend all marinade ingredients. Pour over pork belly slices and refrigerate for minimum 1 hour. Just before cooking, slice chillies and spring onions diagonally, pointy cabbage horizontally. ***Cooking:*** (See FAST COOKING-WOK on page 83) Heat wok to smoking hot with a drizzle of olive oil. Take out pork slices and dry on paper towel. Stir fry pork in small batches until Maillard Brown. Remove browned meat and put in bowl. Just before serving, add more oil to wok and fry chillies, spring onions and pointy cabbage for 1-2 minutes. Return meat to wok. Put in leftover marinade and let thicken (add wine if necessary). You want some thick liquid. Season carefully to taste. ***Serving/Plating:*** Serve on top of a bowl of rice. (See COOKING RICE on page 74) Top with coriander and added chillies if desired. Accompany with seasoned crispy seaweed (or to be authentic, some kimchi).

As a veteran of 2½ years in Seoul, I can say this is a slightly tempered version, with less garlic. Adjust the heat to taste.

Notes

고추장
GOCHUJANG PORK BELLY
POINTY CABBAGE | RED ONION

BONE MARROW CHEESEBURGER

The rich relative of an American classic

  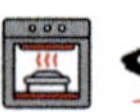     

MAIN | AMERICAN | PREP | GRIDDLE | FAST COOKING | 40m | BEEF | NOT SPICY | EASY

Description:

A far cry from Mickey D's. Prime 5% minced beef made rich by adding bone marrow, worcestershire sauce, mustard and served breadless on a Jack Hawkins or beefsteak tomato base. Not one to pick up with your hands, but juicy and rich.

Ingredients

- Minced beef (5% fat)
- Sea Salt and Black Pepper
- Bone Marrow bones x 2
- Worcestershire sauce (1 tblsp)
- English mustard (1 tblsp)
- Vintage Cheddar
- Jack Hawkins or beefsteak tomato
- Button or chestnut mushrooms
- Bib lettuce
- Avocado

Sauce rose

- Mayonnaise (2 tblsp)
- Greek Yoghurt (2 tblsp)
- Ketchup (1 tblsp)
- Jalapeño Sauce
- Red wine vinegar (1 capful
- Sea Salt and Black Pepper
- Olive Oil

Tools

- Glass Bowl
- Griddle Pan
- Chef's Knife
- Spatula
- Metal ring (large)

Steps

Prep: Preheat oven to **175°C** (325°F). Season marrow bones and roast for 10-15 minutes. Let cool. Mix minced beef, worcestershire sauce, mustard, scooped-out marrow, sea salt and pepper and massage through the meat. Make into a patty using metal ring and then flatten with a metal spatula. Chop, season, and sauté mushrooms for 10-15 minutes until coloured. Reserve in bowl with their juices.

Cooking: Heat griddle pan to screaming hot. Massage a little olive oil on the patties and season again. Cook 3½ minutes a side. After first turning, drizzle jalapeño sauce and olive oil on top. Put sliced cheddar on each patty and cover pan with some foil for the second side for another 3½ minutes. Throw mushrooms in for the last minute.

Plating: Thickly slice a Jack Hawkins. Season and drizzle olive oil on the tomato. Place the burgers and mushrooms on top. Serve sauce in a ramekin to the side to allow diners to spoon on themselves. Accompany with bib lettuce and diced avocado. The ***sauce rose*** doubles as a salad dressing..

These burgers are major-league juicy, and are a distant cousin to the bog-standard patty. The bone marrow adds richness and replaces fat, and the worcestershire sauce and mustard add bite. Of course, you have to eat it with a knife and fork, but your waistline will thank you.

Notes

BONE MARROW
CHEESEBURGER
JACK HAWKINS BUN

IRISH STOUT LAMB STEW

MAIN | BRITISH | HOB | OVEN | SLOW COOKING | 3.5hrs | LAMB | MILD | EASY

Couldn't find a single of Guinness, but any stout will do

Description:

Okay, so it perhaps should have an Irish flag, but all the ingredients of this velvety substantial stew are British save the stout. And the lamb was Welsh and the mashed cauliflower a nice substitute for Irish spuds!

Ingredients

- ◊ Lamb shoulder
- ◊ Carrot x 1
- ◊ Celery Heart x 1
- ◊ Red onion x 1
- ◊ Leek x 2
- ◊ Worcestershire sauce (1 tblspn)
- ◊ English mustard (1 tblsp)
- ◊ Ponzu sauce (1tblsp)
- ◊ Tomato paste (2 tblsp)
- ◊ Smoked Paprika (1 tblsp)
- ◊ Peperoncino paste(1 tblsp)
- ◊ Flour
- ◊ Sea Salt and Black Pepper
- ◊ Parsley
- ◊ Whole head of cauliflower, cut into small flore
- ◊ Greek Yoghurt
- ◊ Grated Parmesan

Tools

- ◊ Casserole
- ◊ Glass Bowl
- ◊ Knife
- ◊ Silicon Spoon

Steps

Prep: Preheat oven to **140°C (284°F).** Cut shoulder into big chunks and remove gristle and obvious tough bits. Equally chunky, dice ***mirepoix*** or ***sofritto*** of carrots, celery, leeks and onions. Boil cauliflower, drain in colander and let dry. Blend together with yoghurt, grated parmesan, olive oil (drizzled in), sea salt,pepper and peperoncino in blender until smooth. In a plastic bag, mix flour, sea salt, pepper, and smoked paprika. Put in the lamb in batches and shake the bag to coat evenly.

Cooking: On high heat on the hob, Maillard brown the lamb without crowding the pan. Drizzle olive oil in the pot and put in the ***mirepoix*** to sweat, stirring constantly. Return the lamb to the casserole, add the stout, worcestershire sauce, mustard, ponzu, tomato paste, and peperoncino paste. Season and cover tightly with foil and lid. Put in oven for 3 hours, stirring occasionally (2-3 times should do it). Remove and let sit for a few hours before serving.

Plating: Heat up stew and mashed cauliflower before serving in a pasta bowl. Drizzle with olive oil and top with parsley. Serve with salad and a ponzu/rice vinegar dressing.(See MAKING A SALAD DRESSING on page 69)

Keep some bread handy for mopping up operations. Under no circumstances throw out the remainder of the sauce. This is the gravy equivalent of gold dust.

Notes

IRISH STOUT LAMB STEW
CAULIFLOWER MASH
MUSTARD

SMOKED SALMON SPAGHETTINI

MAIN FUSION HOB 15m SEAFOOD PASTA/GRAIN NOT SPICY EASY

A Greco-Italian fusion seafood pasta

Description:
Combines creamy taramasalata, oak-smoked salmon, and caviar with the thin gauge pasta in a mouth-watering combination done in minutes.

Ingredients

- Spaghettini (1 index finger circle for 2 people
- Oak Smoked Salmon
- Taramasalata (1 small)
- Danish Caviar (1 jar)
- Lime x 2
- Olive Oil
- Sea Salt and Black Pepper
- Parsley
- Butterhead lettuce

Tools

- Knife
- Saucepan
- Colander
- Spoon

Steps

Prep: Slice smoked salmon into mouth-sized pieces. Boil a saucepan of salted water.

Cooking: Cook spaghettini as per instructions on packet. (8-10 minutes). Reserve a teacup of water. Drain in colander and return to pan. Turn off heat. Mix in a container of taramasalata, the smoked salmon, some olive oil, and allow the hot pasta to lightly cook the fish. Loosen with a few dashes of the reserved pasta water.

Plating: Plate mixed pasta in a pasta bowl. Make a quenelle of caviar and place in middle. Squeeze juice of ½ lime and drizzle with olive oil. Season and then scatter parsley on top. Accompany with a chicory salad with a lime and sea salt dressing. (See MAKING A SALAD DRESSING on page 150).

This succulent quick dish proves the adage that in some cases, the simplest and quickest solution is the best. Yummy as a starter or light supper.

Notes

SMOKED SALMON SPAGHETTINI
TARAMA | CAVIAR

SPRING BORSCHT RAVIOLI

Polish or Russian idea with an Italian twist

MAIN FUSION HOB 15m VEGETABLE PASTA/GRAIN NOT SPICY EASY

Description:
A quick visit to bridge that winter interregnum with the unmistakable thrill of spring. 15 minutes is all that separates you from this dish.

Ingredients

- ◊ Fresh ravioli (Ricotta with spinach, or beetroot)
- ◊ Beetroot pickled in vinegar
- ◊ Frozen Peas (1 cup or 500ml)
- ◊ Sour cream
- ◊ Parmesan
- ◊ Peperoncino paste
- ◊ Olive Oil
- ◊ Sea Salt and Black Pepper
- ◊ Chives
- ◊ Baby mixed lettuce leaves
- ◊ Feta cheese
- ◊ Lemon
- ◊ Light soy sauce

Tools

- ◊ Knife
- ◊ Saucepan
- ◊ Deep frying pan
- ◊ Colander
- ◊ Spoon
- ◊ Spice grinder or blender

Steps

Prep: Divide the beet root packet. Cut half of the beets in quarters. Purée the rest in the spice grinder with soured cream, olive oil, salt and pepper, and peperoncino paste. Grate a healthy amount of parmesan. Make a lemon soy dressing for a salad of mixed baby leaves with crumbled feta.(See MAKING A SALAD DRESSING on page 150).

Cooking: In deep frying pan over medium heat, put in puréed beetroot and a cup of frozen peas in pan and stir to heat through (3-4 minutes). Cook ravioli as per instructions on packet in salted water. (2-3 minutes). Reserve a teacup of water. Drain in colander and drizzle with olive oil. Add pasta to pan and toss to coat evenly. Loosen with pasta water if necessary and blend in the grated parmesan. Drizzle in a good glug of olive oil.

Plating: Plate mixed pasta in a pasta bowl. Top with watercress leaves (and chopped chives if desired).

There is literally no excuse not to do this dish, whether you are a meat- eater, a vegetarian, or someone with no time on your hands. This will put a spring in your step, literally.

 *Notes*

SPRING BORSCHT RAVIOLI

SMOKED SALMON FILLET

 MAIN
 BRITISH
 HOB
 FAST COOKING 30m
 SEAFOOD
 NOT SPICY
 EASY

Salmon, potato salad, and fennel- a happy marriage

Description:
Lightly smoked salmon, a new potato salad with yoghurt, mayo, mustard and chives, and citrus fennel is a palate cleanser and a perfect summer supper.

Ingredients

- ◊ Smoked salmon fillets x 2
- ◊ New potatoes
- ◊ Greek Yoghurt (2 tblsp)
- ◊ Feta Cheese (¼ block)
- ◊ Mayonnaise (1 tblsp)
- ◊ Dijon Mustard (1 tblsp)
- ◊ Chives
- ◊ Fennel Bulb x 1
- ◊ Lime x 2
- ◊ Olive Oil
- ◊ Black Pepper

Tools

- ◊ Knife
- ◊ Frying pan
- ◊ Spatula
- ◊ Tongs
- ◊ Saucepa
- ◊ Glass Bo
- ◊ Spoon

Steps

Prep: Halve new potatoes and boil for 8-10 minutes in salted water. Drain in colander. Crumble feta. Slice fennel bulb thinly and reserve to glass bowl. Make a lime salad dressing. (See MAKING A SALAD DRESSING on page 170) Make a creamy dressing for the potato salad with Greek yogurt, feta, dijon mustard, and olive oil. (See MAKING A CREAMY SALAD DRESSING on page 170) When thoroughly mixed, add potatoes, sprinkle chopped chives, cover with cling film and keep in fridge. Mix sliced fennel with lime dressing, cover with cling film and keep in fridge.

Cooking: Pat dry the salmon fillets. Rub olive oil on skin and season liberally. In dry frying pan on medium/high heat, place fillets skin-side down for 4 minutes. Gently check crispness with spatula. Turn and cook other side for 1½ minutes. Using tongs, turn fillets on side for 30 seconds each to colour.

Plating: Plate three elements with a half-slice of lime and drizzle olive oil on top..

Some dishes leave you just this side of full with a pleasantly cleansed palate and the thought that yes...that was good for me.

 *Notes*

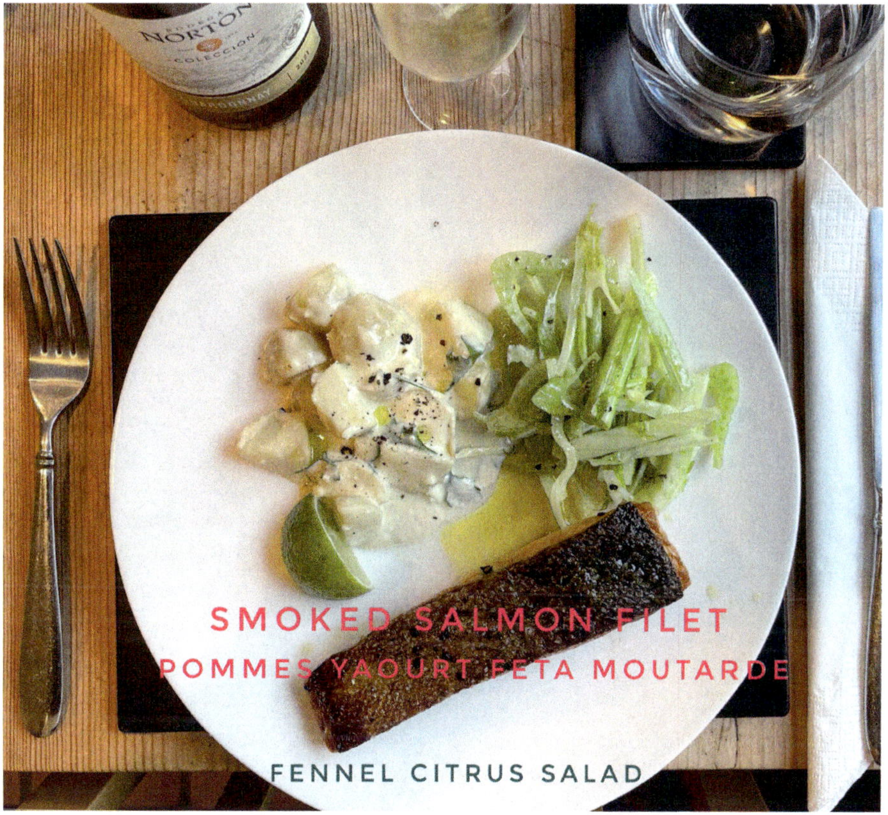

SMOKED SALMON FILET

POMMES YAOURT FETA MOUTARDE

FENNEL CITRUS SALAD

TRIO FRIED RICE

Chicken, Prawns & Pancetta meet in a Chinese classic

MAIN CHINESE WOK FAST COOKING-WOK 25m PORK POULTRY SEAFOOD MILD EASY

Description:
When you can't think of a quick alternative for dinner-this tasty combo of chicken, prawns, pancetta (or lardons), rice and vegetables doesn't miss a beat.

Ingredients

- Chicken Breast (pre-cooked)
- Large Prawns (1 packet)
- Pancetta
- Spring Onions x 4
- Red Chillies x 1
- Sugar snap peas
- Banana Shallots
- Carrot x 1
- Egg x 1
- Coriander
- Rice (½ cup 250ml per person)

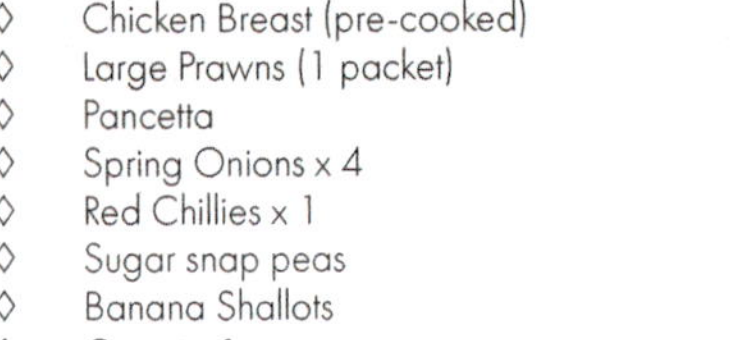

Sauce

- Ponzu (1 tblsp)
- Dark Soy Sauce (1 tsp)
- Rice vinegar (1 tblsp)
- Peperoncino Paste (1 tblsp)
- Lime x 1
- Sea Salt and Black Pepper
- Olive Oil

Tools

- Glass Bowl
- Wok
- Wok Skimmer
- Chef's Knife

Steps

Prep: Well before making this, make some rice and let cool or use leftover rice. (See COOKING RICE on page 74) Slice spring onions, chilli (or chillies), banana shallots, and chicken breast (diagonally). Using parer, make carrot ribbons.

Cooking: Heat wok to screaming hot with a drizzle of olive oil. Stir fry pancetta first to Maillard brown, then chicken pieces, then prawns. Take out browned meat and put in bowl. Add more oil and stir fry onions, sugar snap peas, carrot ribbons and chillies (2 minutes). Crack one egg to side of wok, and once white use the wok stirrer to break apart. Add rice and then add meat back to wok. Put in ponzu, rice vinegar, and peperoncino paste and actively toss/stir to coat evenly.

Serving/Plating: Serve in bowl and top with coriander and added chillies if desired and slice of lime. Drizzle with olive oil. Use chopsticks.

Quick and painless. A great way to a nourishing meal with a bit of bite which combines all of the major food groups in one delicious dish.

Notes

TRIO FRIED RICE
CHICKEN | PRAWN | PANCETTA

RED BEANS & RICE

Stick-to-the-ribs mid-winter stuff

 MAIN  BRITISH  HOB  SLOW COOKING  2hrs  PORK  MILD  EASY

Description:

Perfect for that Sunday afternoon when the weather is awful and you need some proper sustenance to make the day worthwhile.

Ingredients

- Red beans (2 tins)
- Smoked lardons
- ***Mirepoix*** (carrots, celery, red onion)
- Tin of tomatoes (Mutti)
- Guindillas x 2
- Tamed Jalapeños x 4
- Tomato paste (2 tblsp)
- Smoked Paprika (1 tblsp)
- Ground Cumin (1tsp)
- Peperoncino paste(1 tblsp)
- Liquid smoke (1tsp)
- Lime
- Yuzu Shochō paste (1 tsp)
- Red wine (¼ bottle)
- Sea Salt and Black Pepper
- Parsley
- Roquefort
- Greek Yoghurt
- Red wine vinegar
- Fennel
- Pointy Cabbage
- Togarishi (shichimi) powder
- Olive Oil

Tools

- Large deep frying pan with lid
- Glass Bowl
- Knife
- Silicon Spoon
- Spice grinder
- Heat diffuser

Steps

Prep: Dice ***mirepoix*** of carrots, celery, and red onions. Thinly slice fennel stems and pointy cabbage. Drizzle with lime and olive oil and togarashi powder (sparingly). Keep in fridge. Roast cumin and grind along with smoked paprika and sea salt. Make sauce with Roquefort cheese, thick Greek yoghurt, olive oil, red wine vinegar, sea salt and pepper (no mayo). (See MAKING A CREAMY SALAD DRESSING on page 70).***Cooking:*** On high heat on the hob, Maillard brown the lardons. Put in the ***mirepoix*** to sweat, stirring constantly. Add the rest of the ingredients (red wine, tomatoes, tomato paste, spices, peppers, peperoncino paste, liquid smoke, and yuzu shochō). Season and cover tightly with foil and lid. Bring to gentle simmer on heat diffuser for 2 hours, stirring occasionally. Remove lid after 1hr 45min to let sauce thicken. Remove from heat and let sit until 15 minutes before serving and reheat. 25 minutes before serving, make rice. (See COOKING RICE on page 74) ***Plating:*** Serve in bowl on top of rice and top with a healthy dollop of blue cheese sauce. Drizzle with olive oil and top with parsley. Accompany with the fennel and cabbage slaw.

Take your time eating this. You've earned it by waiting.

RED BEANS & RICE
ROQUEFORT YOGHURT CREME
LIME & TOGARASHI FENNEL SLAW

ITALIAN SHRIMP & GRITS

A take on a South Carolina-take on an Italian dish

MAIN | ITALIAN | HOB | FAST COOKING | 45min | PORK | SEAFOOD | MILD | EASY

Description:

Okay, so polenta is different than grits. Distant cousins. But this combination of pancetta and prawns on creamy cheesy salty polenta with a pepper and tomato sauce is a winner.

Ingredients

- Uncooked prawns (1packet)
- Pancetta (cubed or thick rasher)
- Tomatoes x 2
- Tomato paste (2 tblsp)
- Peperoncino Paste (1 tblsp)
- Char-grilled red peppers x 2
- Spring Onions x 4
- Parmesan
- Chilli flakes
- Smoked paprika
- Lime
- Chicken bouillon cube
- Red Wine
- Sea Salt & Black Pepper
- Butterhead or Rosa Verde Lettuce

Tools

- Deep Frying Pan
- Small Frying Pan
- Saucepan
- Knife
- Silicon Spoon

Steps

Prep: Wash and spin lettuce. Halve tomatoes and red peppers. Slice spring onions. Make the tomato/pepper sauce using 2-3 tomatoes, peperoncino paste, red peppers, spring onions, and a glug of red wine, and chilli flakes. Grate parmesan. Boil salted water in saucepan with one bouillon cube for polenta. The ratio of polenta to water should be 5:1. That means for two people, ½ cup (125ml) per person to 2.5cups (625ml) of water.

Cooking: On high heat on the hob in Maillard brown pancetta and add to sauce. Let sauce simmer for 30 minutes. Gradually add polenta to boiling water (think of it as drizzling) while constantly stirring to avoid lumps (15 minutes). Add olive oil and parmesan and chilli flakes and season to taste. Pat and dry prawns. 3 minutes before serving,on high heat, sauté prawns and once coloured (2 minutes), flip and season generously. Top with smoked paprika and lime.

Plating: Spoon polenta into a pasta bowl. Top with sauce and prawns. Drizzle olive oil on top. Accompany with a salad and a vinaigrette.(See MAKING A SALAD DRESSING on page 130)

Creamy and filling, polenta is the European cousin of grits. The joining of pancetta, prawns, peppers and prawns hits the right notes.

Notes

ITALIAN SHRIMP & GRITS
PRAWNS| PANCETTA|POLENTA|PEPERONCINO

STEAK FRITES

Can't get more simple than this bistro favourite

 MAIN  FRENCH  GRIDDLE  FAST COOKING  45m  BEEF  MILD ★ EASY

Description:

When you think steak/frites you might think a Paris bistro with a dijon vinaigrette. You can't provide the bistro, but you sure as hell can replicate the taste. Minimalist with top ingredients. Bon appétit!

Ingredients

- ◊ Sirloin or ribeye steak x 1
- ◊ M&S frites (or Maris Piper for shoestring fries)
- ◊ Butterhead or Rosa Verde Lettuce
- ◊ Lime x 1
- ◊ Green Jalapeño Sauce
- ◊ Dijon Mustard
- ◊ Sea Salt and Black Pepper
- ◊ Olive Oil

Tools

- ◊ Griddle Pan
- ◊ Salad Shaker
- ◊ Tongs
- ◊ Metal Spatulc

Steps

Prep: Preheat oven to **200°C** (400F). Put frites on foil on pizza pan. Season with sea salt. Alternatively, if you have the time, make shoestring fries. (See BLITZED POUSSIN on page 136) Take meat out of the fridge to room temperature (30 minutes) Then rub steak with olive oil and season heavily.

Cooking: Put frites in oven 15 minutes before serving. Heat griddle pan to screaming hot. Cook steak 3.5 minutes each side, and using tongs, 1.5 minutes for the edges (rendering any fat) for medium rare. (See COOKING A STEAK on page 86). Turn the steak, having basted olive oil and green jalapeño sauce on both sides. Remove and cover with foil for ***minimum 5 minutes***. This should coincide with fries crisping up.

Serving/Plating: Trim off excess fat or sinew. Slice thinly across the grain. Squeeze juice of ½ lime and scatter sea salt on top. Accompany with a salad with a dijon vinaigrette.. (See MAKING A SALAD DRESSING on page 69) For authenticity, throw in a glass of red wine.

This is not headline grabbing cuisine, but if done correctly you can transport yourself away to the imaginary bistro on Boulevard St. Germain..

Notes

STEAK FRITES

CHICKEN ESCALOPES

The Viennese would say you stole our schnitzel

MAIN

FRENCH

HOB

OVEN

FAST COOKING

20m

POULTRY

NOT SPICY

EASY

Description:

The French, god love 'em, came up with the chicken escalope to make a little go a long way. And it does. Crispy, moist, succulent. A bite as good as its bark.

Ingredients

- Skinless chicken breasts x 2
- Panko breadcrumbs
- Flour
- Egg x 1
- Tomatoes x 4
- Basil
- Feta
- Chilli flakes
- Lemon x 1
- Bib lettuce
- Dijon Mustard
- Sea Salt and Black Pepper
- Olive Oil

Tools

- Chef's Knife
- Frying pan
- Glass Bowl
- Spatula
- Pounder
- Plastic b---

Steps

Prep: Pat dry chicken breasts. Carefully slice midway lengthwise and fold out to make a thin escalope. Use a sharp knife. Don't worry if they split. Place in a plastic bag on the cutting board and give a gentle bash with the pounder to make them thinner. This will also tenderise them. Crack egg in bowl. In another plastic bag, mix flour, sea salt, pepper, and smoked paprika and shake to mix. Create the salad by slicing the tomatoes thickly, cubing the feta, and picking the smallest leaves from a bunch of basil. Do this before cooking the escalopes. They want to be served hot! On the cutting board, sprinkle bread crumbs, chilli flakes, and more sea salt.

Cooking: Dredge the escalopes in the flour. Dip in the egg to coat evenly, and lay on top of bread crumbs to coat both sides. On a frying pan with ***medium*** heat and a good amount of olive oil, place the escalopes for 2-3 minutes, checking to make sure they are Maillard golden and not burnt. Flip.

Plating: Plate the escalopes, season and squeeze a bit of lemon juice on them. Serve with some dijon mustard and a ½ lemon on side. If desired have a salad with bib lettuce and a vinaigrette.(See MAKING A SALAD DRESSING on page 158)

The key to success is not to burn the escalope and have it golden brown. Precision is required, and the reward worth the attention. You will note the absence of butter. No matter.

Notes

CHARDONNAY
CHICKEN ESCALOPES
POMODORI | FETA | BASILICO

YUZU KOSHŌ FRIED RICE

Yuzu & Chilli Paste Fried Rice with Chicken, Bacon and Cabbage

MAIN

JAPANESE

WOK

FAST COOKING-WOK

25m
PORK

POULTRY

MILD

EASY

Description:
The citrus chilli paste adds an unusual bite to fried rice, with the unmistakable taste of yuzu perfectly matching the heat of green chillies. .

Ingredients

- ◊ Chicken Breast (pre-cooked)
- ◊ Smoked Bacon Rasher x 2
- ◊ Pointy Cabbage x 1
- ◊ Spring Onions x 4
- ◊ Red Chillies x 1
- ◊ Coriander
- ◊ Rice (½ cup 250ml per person)

Sauce

- ◊ Yuzu Koshō Paste (1 tblsp)
- ◊ Sake (1 tblsp)
- ◊ Ponzu (1 tsp)
- ◊ Sea Salt and Black Pepper
- ◊ Dark sugar (1 tsp)
- ◊ Olive Oil

Tools

- ◊ Glass Bowl
- ◊ Wok
- ◊ Spice Grinder
- ◊ Chef's Knife
- ◊ Wok Spoon

Steps

Prep: Well before making this, make some rice and let cool or use leftover rice. (See COOKING RICE on page 166). Slice spring onions, chilli (or chillies), pointy cabbage, bacon, and chicken breast (diagonally). In spice grinder blend all sauce ingredients.

Arrange all ingredients in order of cooking (meat first, spring onions and chillies, sauce, rice,and pointy cabbage last.)

Cooking: Heat wok to screaming hot with a drizzle of olive oil. Stir fry bacon first to Maillard brown, then chicken pieces. Take out browned meat and put in bowl. Add more oil and stir fry onions and chillies (1 minute). Add sauce and stir, then add rice and meat and actively toss/stir to coat evenly. Add pointy cabbage for 1 minute.

Serving/Plating: Top with coriander and added chillies if desired. Serve in bowl with chopsticks.

Yuzu koshō is a relative newcomer to the chef's arsenal, but is versatile and is a wonderful way to wake up those taste buds in fried rice.

Notes

柚子胡椒 FRIED RICE
YUZU KOSHŌ | CHICKEN | BACON

CRAB TORTELLONI

Richness of the brown and white meat with black tortelloni

MAIN ITALIAN HOB FAST COOKING 20min SEAFOOD MILD EASY

Description:

If you can find it, use squid ink tortelloni, but no matter. This is a fast dish which packs a punch of the chilli and lime which cut through the richness of the crab.

Ingredients

- ◊ White crab meat (1 tub)
- ◊ Brown crab meat (1 tub)
- ◊ Lime and lime zest
- ◊ Peperoncino Paste (1tsp)
- ◊ Red chillies
- ◊ Spring onions x 3
- ◊ Sugar snap peas
- ◊ White wine (glug)
- ◊ Parsley
- ◊ Olive oil
- ◊ Sea Salt and Black Pepper
- ◊ (Black) Tortelloni stuffed with crab or ricotta

Tools

- ◊ Deep Frying Pan
- ◊ Small frying pan
- ◊ Saucepan
- ◊ Colander
- ◊ Silicon Spoon

Steps

Prep: Chop spring onions and chilli(es). Zest one lime. In a saucepan boil water and sea salt. Cut any stems off of sugar snaps.

Cooking: On high heat on the hob in deep pan, lightly brown white crab meat (3 minutes) and then add the brown crab, lime zest, chillies and spring onions.(1 minute). Then add a glug of olive oil, white wine, juice of ½ lime and simmer. ***Do not overcook or else the white crab will lose its shape and you will have mush.*** Fry sugar snaps in olive oil in small fryer for 3-4 minutes. Put tortelloni into boil for 2-3 minutes. Drain in colander and drizzle olive oil over the cooked pasta. Return to frying pan and toss to coat evenly.

Plating: Season. Plate the tortelloni in a pasta bowl with sugar snaps on the side. Scatter parsley and drizzle olive oil on top. Accompany with a salad and a vinaigrette.(See MAKING A SALAD DRESSING on page 130)

This is almost an if-you-can-spare-a-moment meal. So quick. So fresh, So rich. So tasty.

Notes

CRAB TORTELLONI AND SUGAR SNAPS

SKIN-STUFFED CHICKEN SUPREME

A juicy alternative to a roast chicken

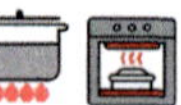

MAIN BRITISH MICROWAVE HOB OVEN MEDIUM 1.5hrs POULTRY MILD MODERATE

Description:

Chicken Supreme is actually a cut of the bird, the breast with the skin on and a bone. This version punches way above its weight.

Ingredients

- ◊ Chicken Supremes x 2
- ◊ Butternut squash (whole or pre-cut)
- ◊ Frozen Spinach cubes (1 pack)
- ◊ ***Stuffing:*** Smoked Lardons (1 pack)
- ◊ Sourdough Bread (
- ◊ Spring Onions x 3
- ◊ Celery sticks x 4
- ◊ Olives with pimentos x 4
- ◊ Red peppers x 2
- ◊ Lime and Zest x 2
- ◊ Satsuma or tangerine
- ◊ Peperoncino paste
- ◊ Yuzu koshō paste
- ◊ Mirin
- ◊ Ponzu
- ◊ Olive oil
- ◊ Sea salt and Black pepper
- ◊ White wine (glug)

Tools

- ◊ Large frying pan
- ◊ Large ceramic flan dish
- ◊ Glass Bowl
- ◊ Masher
- ◊ Blender and Spice Grinder
- ◊ Silicone brush

Steps

Prep: Preheat oven to 175°C (350°F). Dice two slices of sourdough into croutons. Cut squash into small chunks. Dice all other vegetables for stuffing. Reserve to glass bowl. Roast chunks of butternut squash tossed in olive oil and salt and pepper for 40 minutes. Toss croutons in olive oil with sea salt. Roast for 15 minutes on foil on lower shelf. Put squash in saucepan with a 150ml of water and a chicken stock cube. Simmer. Mash. Blitz in blender. Season. Put in ramekin with parmesan on top. Turn oven up to **240°C** (464°F). Sauté lardons, then onions, celery, olives, and red peppers. Mix all stuffing ingredients in a glass bowl with croutons, drizzling with olive oil, zest and juice of ½ lime, peperoncino paste, and sea salt and pepper. In spice grinder blend the yuzu paste, mirin, and ponzu. Skin stuff the supremes by gently prying skin loose with your fingers and jamming in the stuffing (gently in small batches). On the underside, peel back the breast if there is a nugget (or slice the breast) to create a pocket and stuff. Pin with skewer. ***Cooking:*** Maillard brown the supremes, turning carefully and seasoning liberally. In large flan dish, drizzle olive oil, spring onions and leftover stuffing on bottom and place supremes on top. Using a silicon brush, baste entire supreme with the yuzu sauce. Squeeze satsuma and lime on top. Add splash of white wine. Cook for 23 minutes in hot oven, basting twice more with yuzu sauce. Put frozen spinach in glass bowl. Microwave for 6 minutes. Mash out all water. 2 minutes before plating squeeze lime, drizzle olive oil and season. ***Plating:*** Halve the supremes. Top with extra stuffing and gravy. Lay with cut side (or sides). Put spinach in ring and arrange in center of plate. *Delectable!*

SKIN-STUFFED
CHICKEN SUPREME
BUTTERNUT SQUASH | SPINACH

LAMB TAGINE

MAIN | MOROCCAN | HOB | OVEN | SLOW COOKING | 3.5hrs | LAMB | MILD | EASY

Moroccan-inspired dish combining all of the five tastes

Description:

Straight from the streets of Marrakech or the High Atlas mountains, this slow-cooked wonder allows all of the tastes (sweet, sour, spicy, salty, bitter) to meld.

Ingredients

- ½ Lamb shoulder (for two people)
- Carrot x 2
- Red onion x 1
- Shallots x 2
- Baby Leek x 1
- Olives stuffed with pimentos
- Pitted prunes
- Tomato paste (2 tblsp)
- Smoked Paprika (1 tblsp)
- Peperoncino paste(1 tblsp
- Ginger (Thumb-sized knob)
- Cloves x 4
- Turmeric (1 tsp)
- Garlic (1 clove)
- Red wine vinegar
- Cumin seeds/Coriander seeds/Mustard seeds
- Cinnamon (1 stick)
- Flour
- Sea Salt and Black Pepper
- Olive Oil
- Greek Yoghurt/ Mayo/ Dijon mustard
- Cucumber
- Cous cous (1 cup/500ml)
- Sherry or white wine

Tools

- Tagine
- Glass Bowl
- Knife
- Silicon Spoon
- Pestle & Mortar/Spice Grinder

Steps

Prep: Preheat oven to **150°C (300°F).** Cut shoulder into big chunks and remove gristle and obvious tough bits. Slice all vegetables into diagonal chunks. In pestle & mortar, grind garlic, clove and ginger with vinegar and salt and olive oil. Roast and grind all dry spices in spice grinder. In plastic bag, mix flour, sea salt, pepper and spices and shake to coat lamb evenly. De-seed and chop cucumber and mix with yoghurt, mayo, dijon, vinegar, olive oil and cumin seeds. ***Cooking:*** On high heat on the hob, Maillard brown the lamb without crowding the pan. Remove and de-glaze with sherry. Mix all ingredients and put in tagine. Fill halfway up with water. Put in oven for 2½ hours. Five minutes before serving, put in 1:1 ratio of cous cous into boiling water, turn off heat and leave covered. ***Plating:*** In pasta bowl, serve cous cous with lamb on top. Drizzle with olive oil and top with coriander or chopped chives.

Bon appétit! Rock the casbah!

Notes

LAMB TAGINE

DUCK LEGS & PUY LENTILS

Slow and Easy,, simple but complex.

MAIN

FUSION

OVEN

SLOW COOKING

2.5hrs

FOWL

MILD

EASY

Description:

Rich yet light, the melding of a variety of spices from over the world, the sweet, the salty, the umami, and sour make this a perfect easy afternoon's cooking with little

Ingredients

- Duck Legs x 2
- Puy Lentils
- Shallots x 4
- Spring Onions x 2
- Celery sticks x 6
- Apple x 1
- Carrot x 1
- Guindilla Peppers x 2
- Mandarin or Satsuma x 2
- Lime x 1
- Celery salt
- Ponzu (1tblsp)
- Light Soy Sauce (1tsp)
- Peperoncino Paste

For basting sauce

- Pickled Ginger (Kozami)
- Yuzu koshō
- Dark soy
- Sea Salt and Black Pepper
- Olive Oil

Tools

- Knife
- Glass Bowl
- Medium-sized roasting tin
- Apple Core
- Parer
- Tongs

Steps

Prep: Preheat oven to **160°C** (320°F). Core and peel apple and cut into chunks. Finely chop carrot, celery, guindilla peppers, and spring onions. Combine with puy lentils in roasting tin. Put in ponzu, white wine, olive oil (glug), light soy, celery salt, and peperoncino paste and mix well. In spice grinder, combine the pickled kozami ginger, yuzu koshō, olive oil, dark soy sauce into thickish paste. Reserve. Pat dry the duck breasts. Season underside with sea salt and pepper. Place on top of lentils, skin side up. Squeeze juice of one lime and two mandarins. Season again with sea salt and twist of pepper. Drizzle olive oil on top. ***Cooking:*** Put in oven on middle shelf uncovered for 1.5 hours. Take out and with basting brush paint on the basting sauce on both top and bottom. Return to oven for 30 minutes. Keep an eye on the colouring. Everything should be a deep brown, but not burnt in any way. There would be a thickish sauce.

Assembly/Plating: Rest for five minutes. Plate the duck leg with a healthy dose of lentils in a cake ring. Accompany with the simplest of salads at the side and a vinaigrette to cut through the richness. (See MAKING A SALAD DRESSING on page 69) *Sumptuous. No other word for it.*

Notes

DUCK LEG | PUY LENTILS

WHITETIGER
FOOD DREAMS

DESSERTS

TARTE AUX PRUNES

Plum tart in the classic French style

 DESSERT
 FRENCH
 OVEN
 HOB
 MEDIUM COOKING
 30m
 FRUIT
 NOT SPICY
 MODERATE

Description:
This plum tart is straight out of a brasserie on a boulevard, with crisp pastry and a spicy tangy sweetness with a hint of the spices of the east.

Ingredients

- ◊ Puff Pastry
- ◊ Plums x 12
- ◊ Lemon and Zest x 1
- ◊ Brown Sugar (½ cup)
- ◊ Unsalted Butter (100g)
- ◊ All-purpose flour
- ◊ Creme Fraiche
- ◊ Garam Masala (1tsp)
- ◊ Cinnamon (1tsp)
- ◊ Nutmeg (½ nut grated)
- ◊ Sea Salt
- ◊ Apricot Jam

Tools

- ◊ Tarte pan
- ◊ Frying Pan
- ◊ Glass Bowl
- ◊ Baking Beans
- ◊ Spatula
- ◊ Fine gauge Sifter

Steps

Prep: Pre-heat oven to **210°C**(410°F). Make a pastry base using ready-made puff pastry and chill. (See CRISP PASTRY on page 67) Cut all the plums in half and remove pips. Save 7-8 to top pie.

Cooking: Blind bake pastry shell for 15-20 minutes. Rub butter on hot shell when browned sufficiently. After taking out the case, turn oven down to **175°C.** In a frying pan, gently simmer rest of plums, butter, brown sugar, zest and juice of one lemon, garam masala, cinnamon, nutmeg and pinch of sea salt until softened (15-20 minutes on low heat). Depending on consistency, sift in one tsp of flour and blend. Pour filling on top of case and spread evenly. Arrange reserved plums on top. Put pats of butter and pinches of sugar. Bake 35-40 minutes at 175°C, checking occasionally to make sure pastry is not burning. Once pie is done, bring apricot jam (¾ of jar) to a boil, and though a strainer, drizzle ***just the liquid sugar*** all over the tarte to make a glaze.

Serving: Whip brown sugar and creme fraiche together and place a dollop to the side of each slice of the tarte when you serve (with a sprig of mint or holly on the side, depending on the season).

A crispy and tart tarte (pardon the pun) which does the ingredients proud.

 *Notes*

TARTE AUX PRUNES

BERRY AND GINGER NUT

Quick, tasty solution to the what-can-I-make-for-dessert?

DESSERT | BRITISH | NO COOKING | 30m | FRUIT | NOT SPICY | EASY

Description:
A quick last-minute dessert which has a nice blend of the bite of the ginger, the tartness of the blackcurrants, and the luxury of whipped cream.

Ingredients

- ◊ Blackcurrants
- ◊ Raspberries
- ◊ Blueberries
- ◊ Brown Sugar (3 tblsp)
- ◊ Cinnamon
- ◊ Lemon and Zest
- ◊ Double cream
- ◊ Ginger nut biscuits

Tools

- ◊ Ramekins
- ◊ Saucepan
- ◊ Mixer

Steps

Prep: Crush biscuits in a pestle and mortar. Place in bottom of each ramekin and tamp down with bottom of a glass. In saucepan, make a conserve with blackcurrants, sugar, cinnamon, lemon and zest. Boil gently until juice thickens. Taste to make sure it is sweet enough and let cool.

Assembly: Whip the double cream to peaks, and gradually fold in the blackcurrant conserve. Pour into the ramekins and top with a raspberry and blueberries. Store in fridge until needed.

Serving: Accompany with another ginger biscuit.

Simple and visually stunning. Sweet and tart. Small but perfectly formed.

Notes

BERRY AND GINGER NUT MOUSSE

PUMPKIN PIE

An American classic, with an Asian twist

DESSERT | AMERICAN | OVEN | HOB | MEDIUM COOKING | 1hr | FRUIT | NOT SPICY | MODERATE

Description:
It is hard to conceive of a more typically American dish. This version has an unusual addition in the form of garam masala and puff pastry.

Ingredients

- ◊ Puff Pastry
- ◊ Tin of pumpkin x 1
- ◊ Lemon and Zest x 1
- ◊ Brown sugar (¾ cup)
- ◊ Unsalted Butter (100g)
- ◊ Tin of condensed milk (small)
- ◊ Eggs x 4
- ◊ Small double cream x 1
- ◊ Greek Yoghurt
- ◊ Garam masala (1tsp)
- ◊ Cinnamon (1tsp)
- ◊ Ground ginger (1tsp)
- ◊ Nutmeg (½ nut grated)
- ◊ Sea Salt and Black Pepper

Tools

- ◊ Deep pie pan
- ◊ Glass Bowl
- ◊ Hand Mixer
- ◊ Silicone Spoon

Steps

Prep: Pre-heat oven to **210°C**(410°F). Make a pastry base using ready-made puff pastry and chill. (See CRISP PASTRY on page 67) Separate white from yolks in eggs and reserve whites in a large glass bowl. In another glass bowl, combine the tinned pumpkin. condensed milk, double cream, egg yolks, brown sugar, cinnamon, nutmeg, ginger, and garam masala, a squeeze of lemon and lemon zest, and a pinch of sea salt and twist of pepper. Beat with a hand mixer until smooth.

Cooking: Blind bake pastry shell in the pie pan for 15-20 minutes. Rub butter on hot shell when browned sufficiently. After taking out the case, turn oven down to **175°C** (350°F)**.** Beat egg whites until they peak, and then with a silicon spoon fold carefully into the pumpkin mixture. This will enable the pie to rise (and fall) and will make it very light. Pour mixture into pie pan and cook on a middle shelf for 40-45 minutes until nicely browned.

Serving: Whip brown sugar and Greek yoghurt together by hand(with a splash of brandy if desired) and place a dollop to the side of each slice of the pie when you serve .

A traditional Thanksgiving dessert, brought up-to-date and modified. Something to be thankful for.

Notes

PUMPKIN PIE

LEMON CHEESECAKE

Neither cheese nor cake, this is a tart and sweet marvel of simplicity

DESSERT | BRITISH | NO COOKING | 30m | FRUIT | NOT SPICY | EASY

Description:

More like a posset, this is a very quick delight that can be either prepared hours in advance or almost at the last minute, with a digestive biscuit crust and a creamy filling..

Ingredients

- ◊ Lemons x 3
- ◊ McVities Digestive Biscuits
- ◊ Sweetened condensed milk (1 tin)
- ◊ Double cream (small)
- ◊ Walnuts
- ◊ Honey

Tools

- ◊ Ramekins
- ◊ Mixer
- ◊ Glass bowls x 2

Steps

Prep: Crush digestives in a pestle and mortar. Spoon the mixture into ramekins and tamp down with the bottom of a glass. Zest two of the lemons. Blend the condensed milk, double cream, and juice of all three lemons until thick.

Assembly: Pour into ramekins. Top with a walnut, the lemon zest, and a squeeze of honey. Store in fridge until needed (an hour is sufficient).

Serving: Nothing fancy needed. Simplicity, please.

The crispness of the crushed biscuit (more like a crumble) is perfect counterpoint to the thick creamy not-a-cheesecake.

Notes

LEMON CHEESECAKE

TARTE TATIN

Rustic goodness of apples and pastry

 DESSERT  FRENCH  OVEN HOB  MEDIUM COOKING  1hr  FRUIT  NOT SPICY  MODERATE

Description:

A tarte tatin, whose upside-down nature was supposedly a French innkeeper's sister's attempt to correct a oversight by putting pastry on top, has become a sinfully

Ingredients

- ◊ Puff Pastry
- ◊ Apples (Granny Smith) x 4
- ◊ Lemon and Zest x 1
- ◊ Brown Sugar (½ cup)
- ◊ Unsalted Butter (100g)
- ◊ Creme Fraiche
- ◊ Garam Masala (1tsp)
- ◊ Cinnamon (1tsp)
- ◊ Nutmeg (½ nut grated)
- ◊ Sea Salt

Tools

- ◊ Omelette pan
- ◊ Glass Bowl
- ◊ Spatula
- ◊ Apple corer
- ◊ Parer
- ◊ Silicone Pastry Bru

Steps

Prep: Pre-heat oven to **180°C**(350°F). Make a *cartouche* to fit top of a small omelette pan. (See MAKING A CARTOUCHE on page 76).Core apples using an apple corer. Peel and cut in half horizontally. Lay them out in the pan to make sure they fit snugly, and if necessary, cut bits off. Reserve to a glass bowl and squeeze lemon on them to prevent browning. Cut butter into cubes.

Cooking: Spread out sugar in omelette pan, add a tiny bit of water (50ml) and gradually melt over medium heat, swirling pan. ***Don't use a metal spoon.*** When starting to bubble, (3-5 minutes), add and melt butter. Take off heat. Arrange apples with cut-side up (CAREFUL: MELTED SUGAR IS HOT). Dust cinnamon, garam masala, nutmeg, and lemon zest. Brush tops of apples with melted sugar/butter using a silicone pastry brush. Put *cartouche* on pan, tucking in sides, reduce heat, and let simmer for 15-20 minutes. Remove cartouche and take pan from heat. Roll out puff pastry and cut in circle slightly larger than pan (use an upturned plate for a guide). Place on rolling pin, and then unroll on top of omelette pan. Tuck in sides and prick with fork five or six times to let steam escape. Place on middle shelf in oven for 25-35 minutes until pastry is risen and deep brown. Remove and let cool 10 minutes. Cover with serving plate and dexterously flip. Carefully lift pan off and there you have it!

Serving: Whip brown sugar and creme fraiche together and place a dollop to the side of each slice of the tarte when you serve.

A lucky mistake, if ever there was one. Delicious reheated as a breakfast.

Notes

TARTE TATIN

WHITETIGER
FOOD DREAMS

BREAKFASTS

AVOCADO & FETA ON SOURDOUGH

The classic hipster breakfast at home

FUSION | TOASTER | NO COOKING | 10m | SANDWICH | MILD | EASY

Description:

For when you are sick of cereal, eggs, or a croissant, this will refresh your palate. Slightly spicy avocado (think guacamole without the onion) and feta on sourdough.

Ingredients

- Avocado x1
- Lime
- Jalapeño sauce
- Sea salt & Black pepper
- Olive Oil
- Sourdough Toast
- Orange Juice
- Coffee

Notes

Tools

- Knife
- Potato Masher
- Glass Bowl

Steps

Prep: Peel and de-seed avocado. Crush in glass bowl. Squeeze in juice of 1/2 lime and add jalapeño juice or sauce. Add pinch of salt and a grind of black pepper and mix together. Loosen with olive oil. Spread on sourdough toast and crumble feta on top. Drizzle olive oil on top.

Plating: Eat it. This is not art, this is breakfast..

Simple combination which just works. Salty. Sour. Creamy. Wakes up the palate.

AVOCADO AND FETA ON SOURDOUGH

FANCY A PINT SMOOTHIE

This beats last night at the pub

BREAKFAST

BRITISH

NO COOKING

10m

FRUIT

NOT SPICY

EASY

Description:

The perfect precursor to or replacement for the liquid lunch. A pint glass of goodness: banana, raspberries, grapefruit, orange juice, satsuma, yoghurt, walnut, honey, and wheat germ. Surprisingly filling.

Ingredients

- ◊ Banana x 1
- ◊ Raspberries (½ punnet)
- ◊ Grapefruit x 1
- ◊ Satsuma (or tangerine) x 1
- ◊ Greek yoghurt
- ◊ Walnuts,
- ◊ Honey
- ◊ Wheat germ
- ◊ Orange juice

Tools

- ◊ Knife
- ◊ Spice Grinder
- ◊ Silicone Spoon

The very idea of a supremely healthy alternative is sometimes off-putting. This simple breakfast, done in minutes, sets you up for the whole day, and makes you feel good about yourself. Fancy a pint?

Notes

Steps

Prep: Peel and cut all fruit into chunks. Blend in spice grinder (probably need two passes due to the size). Blend in yoghurt and honey and loosen with OJ. Pour in pint glass and put in walnuts and wheat germ and drizzle honey on top.

Plating: None needed. Drink or spoon it in.

FANCY A PINT?
YOGHURT SMOOTHIE
BANANA | RASPBERRY | TSATSUMA | GRAPEFRUIT | WALNUT

CHORIZO, EGG & CHEESE

Hispano-British on toast to start the day

BREAKFAST | BRITISH | FRYING | FAST | 10m | PORK | MILD | EASY

Description:
Spanish chorizo (always mispronounced in the UK as choritzo??), English cheddar, and a fresh egg on sourdough. What could be simpler?

Ingredients

- Sourdough toast
- Vintage Cheddar
- Thinly sliced chorizo x 8
- Egg x 1
- Sea salt and Black pepper

Notes

Tools

- Frying pan
- Spatula
- Knife

Steps

Prep: Slice one slice of sourdough. Slice three piece of cheddar.
Cooking: Fry Chorizo until slightly browned and fat has been rendered. Remove from pan and place on kitchen towel to drain. In chorizo oil, fry egg until sunny side up and place cheddar on top. When almost done (2-3 minutes) half-fold over.
Plating: Put toast in center, layer chorizo and egg and you're away.!

Eggs, toast, OJ, and coffee. Nothing new here except a Spanish twist to put the shine in your morning.

CHORIZO & EGG
HALF-OVER EASY

CHILLI MARMITE CODDLED EGG

Chilli Marmite, Cheddar, and a coddle egg on sourdough toast

BREAKFAST

BRITISH

HOB

FAST COOKING

10m

VEGETABLE

MILD

EASY

Description:
A marriage of umami distant relatives, a runny egg, sharp cheddar and that love-it-or-hate-it wilful cousin-Marmite with a extra pop of chilli. This is a reminder of just how good some British products can be.

Ingredients

- Sourdough toast
- Vintage Cheddar
- Chilli Marmite
- Egg x 1
- Sea salt and Black pepper

Tools

- Silicone Egg coddler
- Frying pan with cover
- Knife

Steps

Prep: Fill frying pan with 1-2 inches of water. Line Egg Coddle with a drizzle of olive oil. Crack egg into coddler and season. Slice a piece of sourdough bread.

Cooking: Bring water in pan to boil, then turn down heat to a gentle boil and cover with lid on for 4-5 minutes. Toast the bread and once toasted drizzle olive oil on it. Spread Chilli Marmite. Slice vintage cheddar and place on toast. Once the egg is done (it should look translucent), slide onto toast. Another drizzle of olive oil and a sprinkle of sea salt and pepper, and ***et voilà!!***

Plating: Put toast in center and have with your OJ & coffee (not pictured)!

Wakey wakey to an umami taste sensation!

Notes

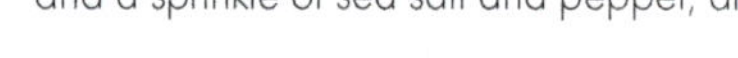

CODDLED EGG
CHEDDAR | CHILLI MARMITE

WHITETIGER
白大虎
FOOD DREAMS

LUNCHES

GRILLED HAM & CHEESE WITH CHILLI PICKLE

LUNCH | BRITISH | HOB | FAST COOKING | 10m | SANDWICH | MILD | EASY

A descant on classic and well-worn tune

Description:
Sourdough grilled ham & cheese. Nothing could be more common. But the devil is in the details, and addition of dijon, mayo and chilli pickle gives the oozy cheese some bite.

Ingredients
- ◊ Sourdough (two slices, not too thick)
- ◊ Thick Ham Slices
- ◊ Vintage Cheddar
- ◊ Sweet Jalapeño Chilli Pickle
- ◊ Dijon Mustard
- ◊ Mayonnaise
- ◊ Olive Oil

Tools
- ◊ Knife
- ◊ Frying Pan
- ◊ Spatula

Steps
Prep: Slice two semi-thick pieces of sour dough. Spread mayonnaise lightly on one side, dijon mustard on the other. Arrange ham and thick slices of cheddar. Then add some chilli pickle
Cooking: Lightly oil the frying pan. Turn flame on medium/low. Put in sandwich, and using the flat spatula, press down on the top to ensure all comes in contact with the heat. After 2-3 minutes, flip and repeat. Better to flip early and keep turning than to have it burnt.
Plating: Slice it in half, and accompany with a pickle or olives, or both. I would avoid crisps, as very quickly you can equal the calories in the sandwich without even realising it.

The doctor might not agree, and you don't want to eat this every day, but some days this is just what the doctor ordered.

Notes

GRILLED HAM & CHEDDAR
SWEET JALAPEÑO CHILLI

SNOOKER SANDWICH

A bit of fun to liven up the Crucible of lunchtime

LUNCH

BRITISH

TOASTER

FAST COOKING

10m

SANDWICH

NOT SPICY

EASY

Description:
It's not so much about what goes on the sandwich, but just as much about whether it makes you smile. Paté. Cheese. Tomatoes. Bog-standard fare, but amusing. And when you're smiling, you're enjoying your food.

Ingredients

- ◊ Sourdough toast
- ◊ Brussels Paté
- ◊ Vintage Cheddar
- ◊ Mixed Baby tomatoes x 8
- ◊ Pimento-stuffed olives x 6
- ◊ Mayonnaise

Tools

- ◊ Knife

If you can't have a bit of fun in the middle of the day, what is the point?

Notes

Steps

Prep: Halve baby tomatoes. Toast a thickish slice of sourdough. Drizzle olive oil on toast. Thinly spread mayo. Layer a thicker spread of paté, slices of cheddar and linear tomatoes.

Plating: Arrange toast on plate with flat side at the bottom. Add six olives to make the snooker triangle. Drizzle olive oil on top and season.

SNOOKER SANDWICH

SALMON TARAMA CAVIAR SKAGEN

A twist on a Swedish toast, strictly speaking a fusion

LUNCH	SWEDISH	TOASTER	FAST COOKING	10m	SANDWICH	NOT SPICY	EASY

Description:
A little bit of Sweden, a little bit of Greece, a little bit of Denmark, and Asian salad dressing. But a skagen is still a skagen. Supremely healthy.

Ingredients

- ◊ Sourdough toast
- ◊ Smoked salmon
- ◊ Taramasalata
- ◊ Caviar (Danish)
- ◊ Rosa Verde lettuce
- ◊ Lime

For the dressing

- ◊ Rice Vinegar
- ◊ Light soy sauce
- ◊ Sesame Oil
- ◊ Olive Oil
- ◊ Sea salt and Black Pepper

Tools

- ◊ Knife

Steps

Prep: Toast a piece of sourdough. Make salad dressing. (See MAKING A SALAD DRESSING on page 69).
Plating: Arrange toast on plate with lettuce to side. Drizzle olive oil on toast, then spread a thick layer of taramasalata, the smoked salmon, and quenelles of tarama and caviar and drizzle with olive oil. Serve with salad dressing shaker and a ½ lime, and allow the diner to dress both.

The combination of the smoky salmon, the salty and tangy taramasalata, the salty caviar, and the sharp dressing with the sesame nuttiness just works beautifully.

Notes

SALMON | TARAMASALATA
CAVIAR SKAGEN
SESAME SOY DRESSING

BRESAOLA & CUCUMBER PEPPER FETA

Italy meets Greece on an Aegean holiday

LUNCH

FUSION

TOASTER NO COOKING

10m

SANDWICH NOT SPICY

EASY

Description:

Bresaola, Parmesan, Lamb's lettuce, Red Peppers, Feta & Yoghurt. You will feel cleansed and just this side of full by this light combination.

Ingredients

- ◊ Sourdough toast
- ◊ Bresaola (1 packet)
- ◊ Shaved Parmesan
- ◊ Lamb's Lettuce
- ◊ Small cucumber x 1
- ◊ Red Peppers from Jar x 2
- ◊ Greek Yoghurt (1 tblsp)
- ◊ Feta Cheese (¼ of block)
- ◊ Red wine vinegar
- ◊ Olive Oil
- ◊ Sea Salt & Black Pepper

For the dressing

- ◊ Lime
- ◊ Olive Oil
- ◊ Sea salt and Black Pepper

Tools

- ◊ Knife
- ◊ Spice Grinder

Steps

Prep: Toast a slice of sourdough. Thinly slice a ½ cucumber. In the spice grinder, blend red peppers, red wine vinegar, feta, yoghurt, olive oil, sea salt, and black pepper to a thick consistency. Make a lime and olive oil salad dressing. (See MAKING A SALAD DRESSING on page 202).

Plating: Arrange toast on plate. Drizzle olive oil on toast, then spread a thick layer of the feta spread, topped with the cucumber slices. Lay out bresaola, shave some parmesan, and top with lamb's lettuce. Serve with salad dressing shaker and allow the diner to dress both the bresaola and the toast.

The rich salty velvetiness of the bresaola and parmesan (a classic Italian combination) combines with the crunchy sweet/salty freshness of the cucumber with the pepper spread. Yum.

Notes

BRESAOLA | PARMESAN | LAMB'S LETTUCE
CUCUMBER TOAST | PEPPER FETA YOGHURT

FORMULA 1 CHICKEN BURGER

Low fat-high octane taste

 LUNCH  BRITISH  GRIDDLE  FAST COOKING 35m  POULTRY  SANDWICH  MILD  EASY

Description:
Under the bonnet of this turbo-charged low fat burger is a powerful engine of taste. Perfect for a sandwich, or in a quesadilla filling with salad, a full meal.

Ingredients

- ◊ 5% Chicken mince (1 packet)
- ◊ Red Chilli x 1
- ◊ Pecorino Cheese
- ◊ Parma ham or Prosciutto x 3
- ◊ Lime
- ◊ Worcestershire sauce
- ◊ Dijon Mustard
- ◊ Frank's Hot Sauce
- ◊ Sage
- ◊ Chives
- ◊ Sake
- ◊ Olive Oil
- ◊ Sea salt and Black Pepper

For Quesadilla (not pictured)

- ◊ Tortilla or ***Piadini***
- ◊ Baby leaf spinach
- ◊ Cheddar Cheese

Frank's creamy dressing

(See MAKING A CREAMY SALAD DRESSING on page 70)

- ◊ Mayo
- ◊ Greek Yoghurt
- ◊ Ketchup
- ◊ Frank's Hot Sauce

For sandwich

- ◊ Sourdough toast
- ◊ Baby Tomatoes
- ◊ ½ avocado

Tools

- ◊ Knife
- ◊ Griddle Pan
- ◊ Spatula
- ◊ Glass bowl

Steps

Prep: Slice and fry prosciutto/parma ham. Slice chilli pepper thinly at a diagonal. Grind sage in spice grinder with sea salt. Dice chives. Mix all ingredients in a glass bowl, working them all through the meat. Form oblong patties, place on plate, and chill in fridge for 30 minutes. Before cooking massage olive oil onto them and season. ***Cooking:*** In hot griddle pan, cook burgers for 3½ minutes each side, pressing down with spatula to ensure even cooking. Drizzle with olive oil. ***Plating:*** For a lunch, just the half piece of toast topped with an avocado and halved baby tomatoes. For the quesadilla, accompany with a salad. The dressing can be used on both the quesadilla and the salad. *This burger is moist and filled with surprises. Gentlemen, start your engines! The next day any leftover patties can be used in a sandwich (see picture).*

Notes

CHICKEN BURGER

CHORIZO & RED PEPPER QUESADILLA

Crisp, juicy, molten cheese like lava.

LUNCH MEXICAN HOB FAST COOKING 10m SANDWICH MILD EASY

Description:
What's not to like about this Mexican/Spanish fusion lunch? Thinly sliced chorizo, juicy sweet red peppers, silky cheese, and bittersweet rocket.

Ingredients

- ◊ Tortilla
- ◊ Thinly sliced Chorizo (15 slices)
- ◊ Chargrilled Mixed or Red Peppers
- ◊ Cheddar
- ◊ Rocket
- ◊ Lime
- ◊ Olive Oil
- ◊ Sea Salt and Black Pepper

Tools

- ◊ Knife
- ◊ Frying Pan
- ◊ Spatula

Steps

Prep:Lay tortilla flat in dry frying pan. Layer slices of chorizo, peppers, slices of cheddar, and rocket. Squeeze juice of ½ lime. Season. Drizzle olive oil. Fold over.

Cooking: On medium heat, fry tortilla, pressing down with spatula, 3-4 minutes each side until golden brown and cheese and chorizo oil ooze out. The outside should be crisp. Nothing worse than a soggy tortilla.

Plating: Slice it in half, and accompany with a pickle or olives, or both.

Olé! That is all you need to say about this delectable and quick sandwich.

Notes

QUESADILLA
CHORIZO | RED PEPPER | ROCKET

BRATWURST, SAUERKRAUT & JARSLBERG

LUNCH FUSION FRYING FAST COOKING 10m SANDWICH NOT SPICY EASY

Germanic/Danish/Polish hybrid we'll call fusion

Description:
When you fancy a beer keller alternative without the beer or the keller, try this hybrid sandwich of jarslberg, robust polish sauerkraut, and bratwurst.

Ingredients

- Sourdough toast
- Bratwurst x 1
- Sauerkraut
- Jarlsberg cheese
- Dijon mustard
- White wine
- Olive Oil
- Sea Salt and Black Pepper
-

Tools

- Knife
- Spatula
- Frying Pan

Steps

Prep: Toast a piece of sourdough. Halve bratwurst lengthways and then halve both sides crossways.

Cooking: In a frying pan with a small amount of olive oil, cook bratwurst cut side down until maillard browned (2-3 minutes). Flip and put in a decent amount of sauerkraut to the side (wait until meat is browned before doing this). On the cut side, put two slices of jarlsberg to melt. Wait a minute or two, then put in a splash of white wine on the sauerkraut and cover. This will help melt the cheese.

Drizzle olive oil on toast and spread a healthy amount of mustard.

Plating: Arrange toast on plate, and using tongs, place bratwurst and top with sauerkraut. Accompany with sliced pickles,and crisps for a special occasion (none if you're after health).

You can imagine having a beer in the skeller with this, but it is lunchtime, so how about some cranberry juice?

Notes

BRATWURST, JARLSBERG, SAUERKRAUT ON SOURDOUGH

WHITETIGER
白大虎
FOOD DREAMS

SOUPS

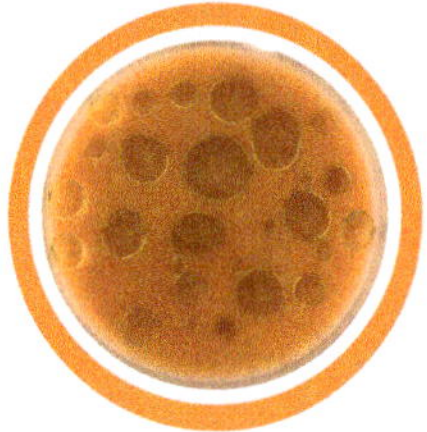

SALMOREJO

The Andalucian version of gazpacho

SOUP SPANISH PREP COOKING 45m VEGETABLE MILD EASY

Description:

This version of salmorejo comes from the restaurant Zoko in Zahara de los Atunes on the Andalucian coast, where the chef revealed a trade secret to make this Andalusian gazpacho thick and creamy (without any cream)

Ingredients

- ◊ Large Tomatoes x6
- ◊ Red Peppers x2 (in jar)
- ◊ Lemon
- ◊ Garlic (1 clove)
- ◊ Chorizo crisps
- ◊ Cucumber (diced)
- ◊ Spring Onions
- ◊ Cream Crackers
- ◊ Sour-dough croutons
- ◊ Peperoncino paste
- ◊ Olive Oil
- ◊ Sea Salt and Pepper

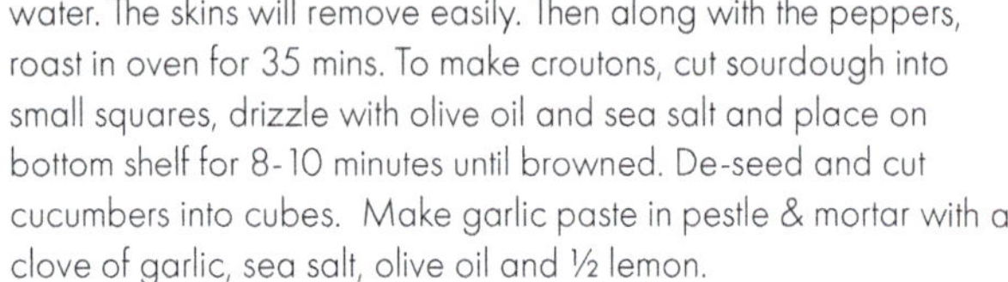

To accompany (optional):

- ◊ Sour-dough Toast
- ◊ Anchovies
- ◊ Manzanilla Olives
- ◊ Feta Cheese

Tools

- ◊ Saucepan
- ◊ Blender
- ◊ Glass Bowl
- ◊ Silicone spoon

Steps

Prep: Preheat oven to **175°C** (350F). Bring tomatoes to a boil in a pot of water. When the skins split, plunge the tomatoes into ice water. The skins will remove easily. Then along with the peppers, roast in oven for 35 mins. To make croutons, cut sourdough into small squares, drizzle with olive oil and sea salt and place on bottom shelf for 8-10 minutes until browned. De-seed and cut cucumbers into cubes. Make garlic paste in pestle & mortar with a clove of garlic, sea salt, olive oil and ½ lemon.

Assembly: Allow the tomatoes and peppers to cool, then put in blender along with olive oil, sea salt, zest of one lemon, garlic paste, ½ cup of water, and 3-4 cream crackers (the trade secret) and whizz until the desired smoothness. Taste and add peperoncino paste and a squeeze of lemon and seasoning. Chill until ready to be served.

Plating: Serve with drizzled olive oil and croutons, crisps, and cucumbers (and thinly sliced spring onion tops). with sourdough toast topped with chopped manzanilla olives (***Fragata*** is a good make), ***Ortiz*** (or other high quality) anchovies, and crumbled feta.

Notes

SALMOREJO
CROUTONS | CHORIZO CRISPS
SOURDOUGH TOAST AVOCADO ANCHOVIES

PONZU PORK UDON

A perfect marriage of rich broth, noodles and pork

SOUP

JAPANESE

FAST COOKING

20m

PORK

MILD

EASY

Description:

This Japanese dish benefits also from some Korean influences, including the ready-made thinly sliced pork belly and the seasoned crispy seaweed on the side. The citrus ponzu marries perfectly with the sweet mirin and sake, the salty dashi, the umami soy, and the browned pork belly.

Ingredients

- ◊ Thinly Sliced Pork Belly (available at Oseyo)
- ◊ Baby Leeks
- ◊ Bak Choi
- ◊ Udon Noodles
- ◊ Dashi Sachets
- ◊ Ponzu
- ◊ Dark Soy Sauce
- ◊ Mirin
- ◊ Sake
- ◊ Pickled Ginger
- ◊ Shichimi Togarashi (spiced seasoning)
- ◊ Olive Oil
- ◊ Sea Salt and Black Pepper

To accompany:

- ◊ Seasoned Seaweed

Tools

- ◊ Deep Saucepan
- ◊ Griddle Pan
- ◊ Glass bowl.
- ◊ Tongs

Steps

Prep: Finely dice baby leeks. Chop the *bak choi* into bite sized pieces. Pat dry the frozen rolls of pork on paper towel, trying to remove as much moisture as possible.

Cooking: In a screaming hot griddle pan, maillard brown the rolled pork belly slices. When they are browned, toss in dark soy sauce to add further colour. Remove to glass bowl. In the deep saucepan, sweat the baby leeks (3-4 minutes). Then add 250ml (1cup) of water ***per person***, and large glugs of ponzu, mirin, sake, and a dashi sachet and once boiling, turn heat down to simmer. Just before serving, turn heat up, add udon noodles, *bak choi*, and pork and let boil vigorously for a minute.

Plating: Serve in bowls with chopsticks and a spoon. Top with pickled ginger and sprinkle on the shichimi *togarashi*. ***Shichi*** means seven, ***mi*** taste and is the chilli seasoning found at your table in most Japanese restaurants. Drizzle a little olive oil. Accompany with the seasoned seaweed .

Citrus hints, spicy, umami, succulent pork, and the slurpable udon make this a terrific dinner. (By the way, it is perfectly acceptable to finish off the broth by more slurping from the bowl.)

Notes

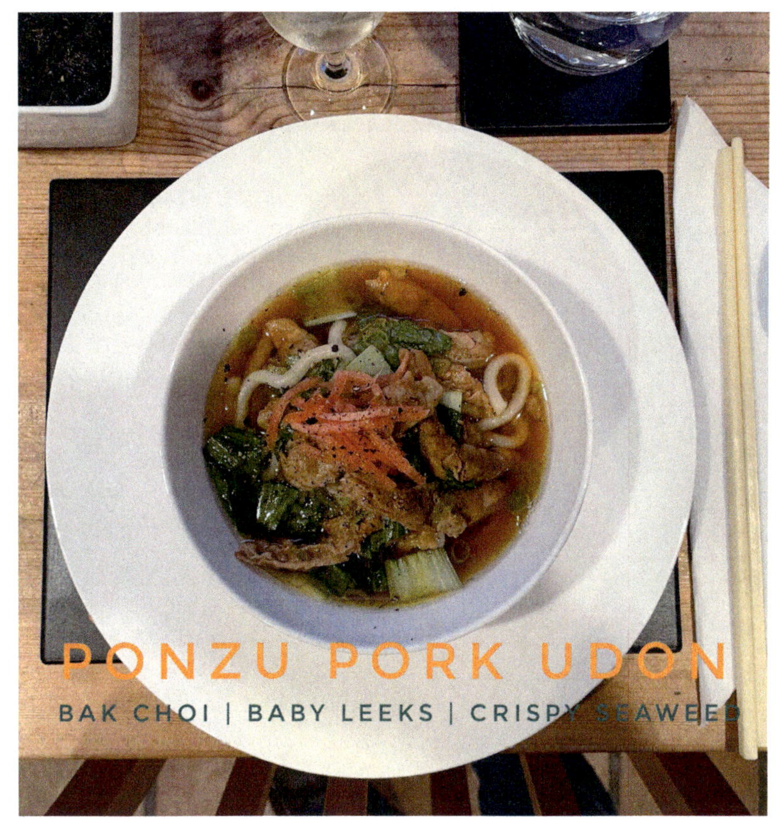
PONZU PORK UDON
BAK CHOI | BABY LEEKS | CRISPY SEAWEED

SOPETTA SCARPETTA

A made-up name for a made-up soup

 SOUP  FUSION  FRYING OVEN  FAST COOKING  30m  PORK  MILD  EASY

Description:

*Okay, so there is no such word in either Spanish or Italian called **sopetta.** And scarpetta means 'little shoe.' But in Italian fare la scarpetta means to mop up everything in a dish with a piece of bread. And that is what you will do with this chorizo and puréed butter bean Italo-Spanish soup/stew concoction.*

Ingredients

- ◊ Chorizo Picante
- ◊ Butter beans
- ◊ Shallots x 3
- ◊ Celery stalks x 4
- ◊ Manzanilla olives
- ◊ Guindilla peppers x 2
- ◊ Pome dei Moro or cherry tomatoes on the vin
- ◊ Lemon x 1 and Zest
- ◊ Garlic (1 clove)
- ◊ Rosemary (1 stem)
- ◊ Red wine (glug)
- ◊ Olive Oil
- ◊ Sea Salt and Black Pepper
- ◊ Flat Leaf Parsley

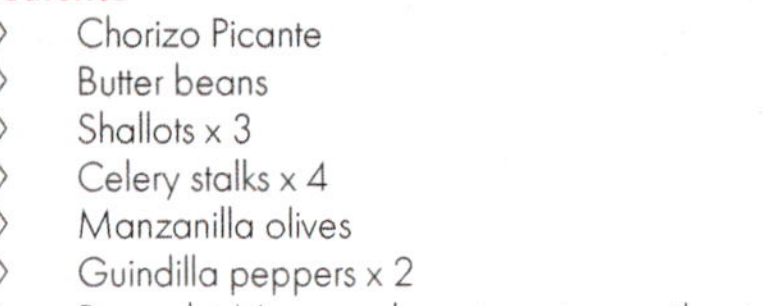

To accompany:

- ◊ Pain de campagne or ciabatta rolls or toast

Tools

- ◊ Knife
- ◊ Ceramic Flan dish (large)
- ◊ Blender

Steps

Prep: Preheat oven to **240°C** (464°F). Slice chorizo into small chunks. Dice celery, shallots and guindillas. In small copper pan, gently confit in olive oil a clove of garlic (whole but partly crushed), lemon zest, and rosemary twig to infuse the oil. After 10 minutes, turn off heat and chuck out ingredients. In blender, liquidise a tin of butter beans, juice of 1 lemon, the flavoured oil, grated parmesan, salt and pepper until very smooth. Add water or more olive oil to get right consistency.

***Cooking*:** Maillard brown chorizo, enough to render fat, and then chuck in celery, shallots, and a glug of red wine. Turn off heat. Combine all ingredients in ceramic dish, (including the tomatoes still on vine) and cook in oven for 23 minutes. Toast bread or heat rolls until outside is crisp.

Plating: Serve in pasta bowls with a good amount of chopped parsley. Accompany with a salad with a vinaigrette, the rolls and some olive oil for drizzling. (See MAKING A SALAD DRESSING on page 69)

*Have spoons to eat and bread handy for mopping up operations. Remember: **Fare la scarpetta!***

Notes

SOPETTA SCARPETTA

ZUPPA DI COZZE

Mussel soup. Dream of being in Sardinia

SOUP | ITALIAN | FAST COOKING | 30m | SEAFOOD | MILD | EASY

Description:

This Italian soup marries the taste of the sea and the land: il mare e la terra. With bread for dipping, this is a meal in itself. All that is missing is a crystalline sky and the smell of the Mediterranean and the sun-burnt Sardinian hills.

Ingredients

- Mussels
- Tinned Tomatoes x 1 (***Mutti***)
- Garlic (1 clove)
- Lemon and lemon zest x 1
- Spring Onions
- Peperoncino paste (1 tblsp)
- White wine
- Olive Oil
- Sea Salt and Black Pepper
- Chilli Flakes
- Flat Leaf Parsley

To accompany:

- Pain de campagne or ciabatta rolls

Tools

- Deep Saucepan with Glass lid
- Pestle & Mortar
- Silicone Spoon

Steps

Prep: Preheat oven to **210°C** (*410°F*). Slice spring onions. Crush clove of garlic, juice of one lemon, olive oil, and sea salt in pestle & mortar into a paste. Chop parsley. Rinse mussels thoroughly in a colander under cold water. Discard any that are open. Pick beards off any. Remember this rule: ***Raw open bad, cooked open good.***

Cooking: On high heat, put in spring onions with olive oil and lemon garlic paste for 1 minute. Then tin of tomatoes, peperoncino paste, and chilli flakes. Let simmer 10 minutes. Then turn heat up to high and put in mussels and cover to steam. Boil until they are open (2-3 minutes). Pick out any which stay closed. Remove half of them and pick out meat and discard those shells. Add a glug of white wine and return picked mussels to the pan. Boil vigorously a few minutes. Put *ciabatta* rolls or *pain de campagne* in oven for 5 minutes.

Plating: Serve in bowls with a good amount of chopped parsley. Accompany with a salad with a vinaigrette, the rolls and some olive oil for drizzling.. (See MAKING A SALAD DRESSING on page 69)

No need for a fish stock. This dish flavours itself. Just enough garlic, salt, hints of lemon, a taste of chilli, wine, and most of all, the sea. Keep the bread handy for mopping up. And use good quality olive oil!

 *Notes*

ZUPPA DI COZZE

SPLIT PEA SOUP

Good stick to the ribs stuff

SOUP | BRITISH | FAST COOKING | 45m | VEGETABLE | MILD | EASY

Description:

A great winter/autumn soup with ham hock and new potatoes, which still maintains the vibrant hues of the peas and a subtle pop of a few peas put in at the last moment

Ingredients

- Frozen Petits pois (1 packet)
- Spring Onions
- New Potatoes
- Guindillas x 2
- Ham Hock (pre-cooked)
- Worcestershire Sauce
- English Mustard
- White wine
- Chicken Bouillon cube x 1
- Olive Oil
- Sea Salt and Pepper

To accompany (optional):

- Sour-dough Toast
- A creamy brie (try ***Minger***, a Scottish brie)

Tools

- Saucepan
- Blender
- Glass Bowl
- Silicone spoon

Steps

Prep: Chop the spring onions and guindillas and halve the potatoes.

Cooking: Sweat the onions and guindillas over low heat in a saucepan. Fry the ham hock in a frying pan to Maillard brown, then splash a glug of white wine and turn off heat. Add 750ml (3 cups) of water, ¾ of the packet of the peas, the bouillon cube, mustard and worcestershire sauce and boil for 15-minutes. Let cool for 15 minutes, and then blend in blender until completely smooth. Return to saucepan, add the potatoes and ham hock, and boil gently for 10-15 minutes. This can be done early and left to sit. Just before serving, crank up the heat to a boil and put in the remainder of the peas for 3-4 minutes.

Plating: Either serve with a dollop of sour cream, or if you want to get fancy, put soured cream in a squirt bottle and get artistic. Drizzle with olive oil and accompany with sourdough toast and a decent cheese.

This handy little treat is even better the next day. It thickens even more and the flavours blend even more.

Notes

SPLIT PEA SOUP
HAM HOCK | GUINDILLAS
McGUIGAN
CHARDONNAY
MINGER

CHICKEN NOODLE SOUP

Good for what ails you, and tasty to boot

 SOUP  BRITISH  SLOW COOKING 3.5hrs  POULTRY  VEGETABLE  NOT SPICY EASY

Description:

Grandmothers know a thing or two of both cooking and healing, so you'd best pay attention. This is not to be hurried, but the result is definitely a pick-me-up for your spirits and your health. Perfect if you have a cold.

Ingredients

- Chicken wings
- Carrots x 4
- Red Onion
- Shallots x 4
- Celery sticks
- Lime
- Chicken Bouillon cube x 1
- Ponzu
- Egg noodles
- Olive Oil
- Sea Salt and Pepper

To accompany (optional):

- Ciabatta rolls x 2
- Cheese (cheddar or brie)

Tools

- Deep Saucepan with lid
- Knife
- Glass Bowls
- Silicone spoo

Steps

Prep: Make a ***mirepois/sofritto*** with big chunks of ½ of your celery, 2 carrots and a red onion. The red onion should be quartered. In a separate bowl, slice the remainder of the carrots and celery plus 4 shallots finely, and reserve in fridge.

Cooking: STEP 1: Season and Maillard brown the chicken wings (10 minutes). Reserve to a bowl. Gently sauté the ***mirepoix*** for 4-5 minutes, not colouring. Return the wings to the pot. Fill ¾ full with water. Add lime juice and zest, a boullion cube, a dash of ponzu, and simmer for 2-3 hours at low heat, covered for two hours and stirring occasionally. Remove lid for last hour to concentrate the flavours. ***STEP 2.*** Let cool and drain in colander, catching ALL of the liquid in a saucepan. This is your broth. Skim off any fat. Once cooled, pick the chicken off the bones, and add to the broth. Bin the now-mushy vegetables. If you need more liquid, top up with water. You can let this sit until you are a half-hour out from eating. Add the reserved dainty ***mirepoix*** to the saucepan and let boil (12 minutes) until almost ready to plate. Add egg noodles and cook for 3-4 minutes.

Plating: Drizzle with olive oil, top with parsley and accompany with ciabatta toast and a decent cheese.

Though I cannot actually recall my grandmother making me chicken soup, I am sure she would approve of this production.

 *Notes*

CHICKEN NOODLE SOUP

GRATIN DAUPHINOIS SOUP

Make it with leftover gratin or from scratch

SOUP

FRENCH

PREP

FASTCOOKING

45m

PORK

MILD

EASY

Description:
Ever wonder what to do with leftover potatoes? This hearty soup can be made from fresh ingredients or a gratin dauphinois which has been sitting in the fridge.

Ingredients

- Gratin dauphinois (potatoes, cheddar, cream)
- Spring Onions
- Baby Leeks
- Bavarian Frankfurters x 3
- Guindillas x 2
- Baby leaf spinach
- Soured cream (small)
- Chicken bouillon cube
- Dijon mustard (1 tblsp)
- White wine
- Olive Oil
- Sea Salt and Pepper

To accompany (optional)

- Seeded rye bread
- Cheddar

Tools

- Saucepan
- Frying pan
- Blender
- Glass Bov
- Silicone sp

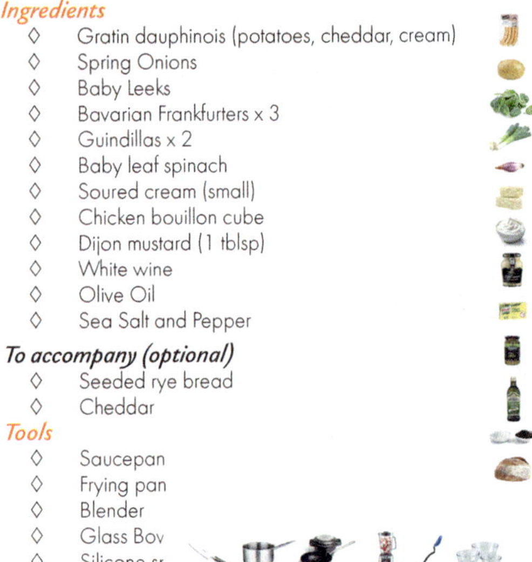

Steps

Prep: Preheat oven to **180°C** (356°F). Chop leeks and guindillas. Slice frankfurters into bite sized pieces. Make croutons from diced sourdough and drizzle on olive oil and sea salt and let brown in oven (10 minutes) Use leftover gratin dauphinois ((See GRATIN DAUPHINOIS on page 124)).*If you have no leftover gratin,* substitute by boiling some diced potatoes for 10 minutes until soft and making a roux with some cheddar. Add that in the next step. All is forgiven in the blender.(See MAKING A ROUX on page 71)

Cooking: Sweat the leeks and guindillas over low heat in a saucepan. Maillard brown the frankfurters in a frying pan, then splash a glug of white wine and sliced spring onions and turn off heat. In another saucepan, add 750ml (3 cups) of water, sour cream, potatoes (and/or roux), bouillon cube, and mustard and boil for 15-minutes. Let cool, and then blend in blender until completely smooth. Return to saucepan, add the frankfurters and spring onions, and simmer gently for 10 minutes. Just before serving, crank up the heat to a boil and put in the spinach for a minute or two until wilted.

Plating: Drizzle with olive oil, top with croutons and grated cheddar and accompany with rye toast and a decent cheese.

Don't let an ingredient go to waste. The humble leftover potato can be elevated from second fiddle to star status with this soup.

Notes

GRATIN DAUPHINOIS SOUP

FRANKFURTER | SPINACH | LEEK

PORK BELLY RAMEN

A 20 minute take on a 24 hour process of this classic dish

SOUP | JAPANESE | FAST COOKING | 30m | PORK | MILD | EASY

Description:

Leave the day long process of creating the perfect pork broth to the professionals. This tasty hack replicates the flavours in a fraction of the time.

Ingredients

- Thinly Sliced Pork Belly (available at Oseyo)
- Baby Leek
- Spring onions
- Bak Choi
- Bamboo Shoots
- Nori
- Egg x 1
- Ramen Noodles
- Either red or light miso paste (2 tblsp)
- Mirin (glug)
- Dark soy sauce (1 tblsp)
- Sake (glug)
- Nori (seaweed)
- Shichimi Togarashi (spiced seasoning)
- Olive Oil
- Sea Salt and Black Pepper

To accompany:

- Seasoned Seaweed
- Tsukemono (pickles-not pictured)

Tools

- Deep Saucepan
- Griddle Pan
- Glass bowl.
- Tongs

Steps

Prep: Slice baby leeks. Chop the *bak choi* into bite sized pieces. Pat dry the frozen rolls of pork on paper towel, trying to remove as much moisture as possible. Slice nori into strips. Finely slice spring onions.

Cooking: In a screaming hot griddle pan, maillard brown the pork belly slices. When they are browned and the fat rendered, toss in dark soy sauce to add further colour. Fry the bamboo shoots to golden. Boil and egg for 6 minutes and plunge in ice water. In a deep saucepan, sweat the baby leeks (3-4 minutes). Then add 250ml (1cup) of water ***per person***, dissolve the miso, soy sauce, mirin and sake and once boiling, turn heat down to simmer. 3 minutes before serving, turn heat up, add ramen noodles, *bak choi*, and pork and let boil vigorously for a minute. Slice egg in half.

Plating: Serve in bowls with chopsticks and a spoon. Place all ingredients on top. Sprinkle on the shichimi *togarashi*. Drizzle a little olive oil. Accompany with seasoned seaweed and/or *tsukemono*. (See PICKLES on page 34)

Indistinguishable (almost) from the real McCoy.

Notes

PORK BELLY RAMEN

CARROT SOUP

Fresh, spicy, deep flavours for such a simple vegetable

  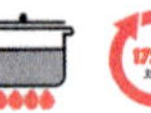    

SOUP BRITISH FASTCOOKING 50m VEGETABLE MILD EASY

Description:
Carrots are like a colour on palette. In a soup, it can take on many colours and tastes--spicy, sweet, umami, as many flavours as there are shades of orange.

Ingredients

- ◊ Carrots x 4
- ◊ Chef's carrots (1 packet)
- ◊ Baby Leeks
- ◊ Celery Sticks x 4)
- ◊ Chicken Bouillon cube x 1
- ◊ Cumin
- ◊ Mustard Seeds
- ◊ Peperoncino paste (1 tsp)
- ◊ Satsuma x 1
- ◊ Sour cream
- ◊ Chives x 1 packet
- ◊ Olive Oil
- ◊ Sea Salt and Pepper

To accompany (optional)

- ◊ Sour-dough Toast

Tools

- ◊ Saucepan
- ◊ Blender
- ◊ Spice Grinder
- ◊ Glass Bowl
- ◊ Silicone spoon

Steps

Prep: Preheat oven to **180°C** (356°F). Chop the baby leeks and celery sticks. Peel and slice the raw carrots. Place on foil, drizzle olive oil, season, and roast in oven for 35-40 minutes. Roast and grind cumin seeds, mustard seeds, and sea salt.

Cooking: Sweat the leeks and celery over low heat in a saucepan, with the spices blended in. Add 2 cups (500ml) of water with a chicken stock cube. Simmer for a bit, and let cool. In the blender, mix roasted carrots with the vegetables, a tablespoon of sour cream, the juice of a satsuma and a tablespoon of peperoncino paste. Whizz until smooth. In a small frying pan, gently sauté the chef's carrots in olive oil , drizzle on some honey and place a *cartouche* over the pan. (See MAKING A CARTOUCHE on page 76) Let cook for 6-8 minutes on medium heat to braise and glaze the carrots.

Plating: Serve in a bowl with 3 to 4 of the glazed carrots on top of the soup. Complete with a dollop of sour cream and some chives. Drizzle with olive oil and accompany with sourdough toast if desired .

 *Notes*

CARROT SOUP

TUSCAN BEAN & SAUSAGE SOUP

Hearty stick-to-the-ribs stuff from this Itallian marvel

 SOUP

 ITALIAN

FAST COOKING

 1hr

 PORK

 MILD

 EASY

Description:

Nothing like this soup on a wintry evening to warm your innards and dream of Tuscany (and oh yes, use up that parmesan rind you have lying around)

Ingredients

- ◊ Calabrian spicy sausage
- ◊ Cannelini beans
- ◊ Spring onions
- ◊ Red Onion x 1
- ◊ Carrot x 1 (large)
- ◊ Celery Heart x 1
- ◊ Baby tomatoes x 6
- ◊ Tomato paste (1 tblsp)
- ◊ Peperoncino paste (1 tblsp)
- ◊ Tin of chopped tomatoes x 1
- ◊ Baby spinach
- ◊ Red wine (1 good glug)
- ◊ Rind of parmesan
- ◊ Olive Oil
- ◊ Sea Salt and Black Pepper

To accompany

- ◊ Sourdough bread
- ◊ Cheeses (cheddar, brie, or Gorgonzola)

Tools

- ◊ Deep Frying pan
- ◊ Glass bowl
- ◊ Spice grinder (for bread if needed)
- ◊ Silicone spoon

Steps

Prep: Remove sausages from their skin and tear into 3cm chunks. Slice spring onions and quarter red onion. Dice carrots and celery into good-sized chunks. Halve baby tomatoes.

***Cooking*:** Maillard brown the sausages for 8-10 minutes on medium high in a lightly-oiled frying pan. Get a good crust on them. Remove to glass bowl and put in celery, onions, spring onions, and tomatoes into frying pan for 3-5 minutes to soften slightly. Return sausages to pan. Add beans (including liquid), glug of red wine, tomato paste, tin of tomatoes, and peperoncino paste and stir. Drizzle with olive oil and season. Cover and let simmer on lowest heat (or heat diffuser) for 25 minutes, then uncovered for 10 minutes. If not thick enough, blitz a piece of sourdough in the spice grinder and add and stir. Season again to taste. A minute before serving, add baby spinach and let wilt.

Plating: Serve in bowls with some sourdough toast and a plate of cheese.

Notes

SOUP
TUSCAN BEAN & CALABRIAN SAUSAGE
TOMATO

WHITETIGER
FOOD DREAMS

SALADS

PINK TRICOLORE

The pink tricolour

 SALAD  FUSION  HEAT SOURCE  NO COOKING  10m  SALAD  NOT SPICY  EASY

Description:
A colourful light salad of multi-coloured tomatoes, red chicory (endive), cottage cheese, with a pink smoked chipotle dressing

Ingredients

- ◊ Mixed baby tomatoes
- ◊ Red endive (chicory)
- ◊ Cottage cheese

Pink Sauce

- ◊ Mayonnaise
- ◊ Greek Yoghurt
- ◊ Red Wine Vinegar (capful)
- ◊ Chipotle Ketchup
- ◊ Sea Salt and Black Pepper
- ◊ Olive Oil

Tools

- ◊ Knife
- ◊ Glass Bowl

Steps

Prep: Halve the tomatoes. Tail the chicory and cut into two segments horizontally. Make the pink sauce in a bowl by blending the mayo, yoghurt, ketchup, and vinegar with a salad fork first and then gradually adding olive oil and seasoning to taste. (See MAKING A CREAMY SALAD DRESSING on page 70)

Assembly/Plating: Place chicory first and then spread tomatoes about, alternating colours. Put a dollop of cottage cheese in the middle, and make a quenelle of the sauce on top.

This comes under the category of few colourful ingredients and little time, but can look (and taste) a masterpiece.

 *Notes*

PINK TRICOLORE

MIXED TOMATOES | RED ENDIVE | COTTAGE CHEESE

SMOKED CHIPOTLE DRESSING

DILL CHICKEN SALAD

Chicken Breast, Carrot and Celery ribbons

SALAD | BRITISH | HEAT SOURCE | NO COOKING | 10m | SALAD | NOT SPICY | EASY

Description:

Vibrant and fresh, this salad has substance and bite. Chicken breast sliced thickly, baby tomatoes, celery and carrot ribbons and capers in a eye-popping green creamy dill dressing

Ingredients

- Chicken breasts x 2 (pre-cooked)
- Mixed baby tomatoes
- Carrot
- Celery Hearts
- Capers (1 tblsp)
- Baby Bib Lettuce

Dill Dressing

- Mayonnaise (dollop)
- Greek Yoghurt (dollop)
- Lime
- Dill
- Sea Salt and Black Pepper
- Olive Oil

Tools

- Knife
- Glass Bowl
- Parer

Steps

Prep: Halve the tomatoes. Create ribbons of celery and carrot using the parer. Make the dressing in a bowl by blending the mayo, yoghurt, lime, and chopped dill with a salad fork first and then

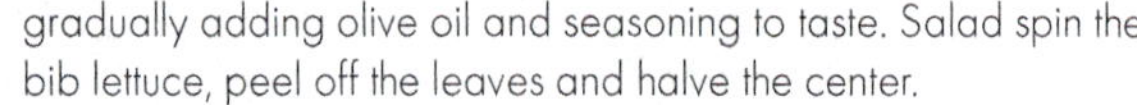

gradually adding olive oil and seasoning to taste. Salad spin the bib lettuce, peel off the leaves and halve the center.

Assembly|Plating: Thoroughly mix all ingredients (save the lettuce) and arrange on the plate with the bib lettuce as pictured. You can either have a long-necked olive oil cruet handy and lime for the salad (or a vinaigrette (See MAKING A SALAD DRESSING on page 69)), with salt and pepper at the ready.

A visual hommage to spring and summer, no matter what the weather. Versatile as lunch, light supper, or starter.

Notes

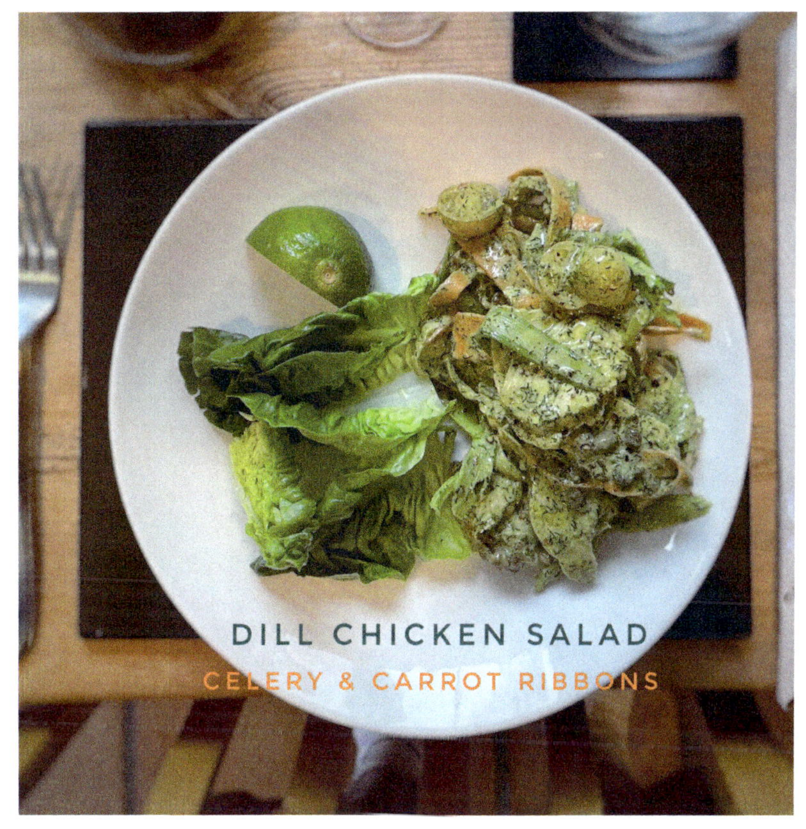
DILL CHICKEN SALAD
CELERY & CARROT RIBBONS

THAI BEEF SALAD

A perfect refreshing way to eat protein and salad at once

SALAD THAI PREP GRIDDLE FAST COOKING 1hr15m BEEF V. SPICY EASY

Description:
A salad which cleanses the palate and sates the appetite with the sour sweet spicy sensation that is Thai food.

Ingredients

- Thick-cut sirloin steak
- Lime x 1
- Red Onion x 1
- Spring onion x 1
- Glass Noodles
- Carrot x 1
- Cucumber x 1
- Bib lettuce
- Red Thai chillies
- Palm or brown sugar (1 tsp)
- Lemon grass stalk x 1
- Garlic (1 clove)
- Thai Fish Sauce (Nam pla)
- Sriracha sauce (a few squirts)
- Chilli flakes
- Sea Salt and Black Pepper
- Olive Oil

Tools

- Saucepan
- Glass Bowl
- Griddle Pan
- Chef's Knife
- Colander

Steps

Prep: Crush ½ stalk of lemon grass, garlic clove, lime juice, sea salt, and olive oil in pestle and mortar to make paste. Make marinade for steak with paste, juice of ½ lime, fish sauce, crushed palm sugar (or brown sugar), sriracha sauce, and one sliced Thai chilli (with seeds). Marinate in fridge for at least ½ hour. Remove 20 minutes before cooking. Using the julienne parer, julienne carrot and cucumber. Finely (and I mean ***finely)*** slice red onion. Boil Thai glass noodles for 2 minutes and then run through cold water in colander. Mix in glass bowl with cucumber, carrot, sugar, lime juice, fish sauce,a Thai red chilli,a dash of sriracha, and finely sliced spring onion. ***Cooking:*** (See COOKING A STEAK on page 86) Heat griddle pan to screaming hot. Remove steak from marinade, reserving the marinade. Pat dry the steak, massage a little olive oil, season and add some chilli flakes. Cook 3½ minutes a side. After first turning, drizzle olive oil on top. Remove and place on cutting board and let rest 15 minutes. ***Plating:*** Slice steak cross-grain at an angle as thinly as possible. It should have a nice bark and be medium rare. Top with reserved marinade and a pinch of sea salt. On little pockets of bib lettuce, place the noodle salad.

The solution for beef eaters to have something beyond steak and potatoes, with the added bonus of a spicy Thai salad.

Notes

THAI BEEF SALAD
GLASS AND CUCUMBER NOODLES

BANG BANG CHICKEN

A spicy cold salad with a Szechuan pedigree

SALAD

FUSION

HEAT SOURCE

NO COOKING

20m

PASTA/GRAIN

MILD

EASY

Description:
A misnomer from the original pounded chicken recipe in China, perhaps, but a delicious salad that blends many different tastes, textures, and ingredients

Ingredients

- ◊ Egg noodles
- ◊ Chicken breasts x 2 (Ready cooked)
- ◊ Carrot
- ◊ Cucumber
- ◊ Coriander
- ◊ Red Chilli
- ◊ Lime
- ◊ Roasted Salted (or Marmite) peanuts
- ◊ Sea Salt & Black Pepper
- ◊ Olive Oil

Peanut Sauce Ingredients

- ◊ Garlic (1 clove)
- ◊ Ginger (1 knob
- ◊ Sesame Oil
- ◊ Marmite Crunchy Peanut Butter
- ◊ Rice Vinegar
- ◊ Mirin
- ◊ Light Soy Sauce
- ◊ Honey (a decent squeeze)
- ◊ Peperoncino Paste (1tsp)
- ◊ Juice of 1 Tangerine
- ◊ Olive OIl

Tools

- ◊ Glass Bowl
- ◊ Cuisinart Spice Grinder
- ◊ Chef's Knife
- ◊ Julienne and regular Parer

Steps

Prep: This recipe uses pre-cooked ingredients (noodles and chicken breasts). You can use leftover chicken pieces or boil quick-cook noodles. Peel, halve lengthwise and de-seed the cucumber and pat dry with paper towel. Peel the carrot. Julienne both and place in large glass bowl. Slice the chicken breasts into diagonal bite size pieces. Thinly slice a chilli (or two). Add the noodles to the bowl. In the spice grinder, combine all the sauce ingredients and whizz. Taste and add olive oil to get a smooth consistency.
Assembly: Combine all in the bowl so that everything is evenly coated.
Plating: Serve in pasta bowl with sprigs of coriander and lime. Drizzle olive oil on top. along with crushed marmite peanuts (optional).

A good light supper or lunch when the British summer shows its face.

Notes

BANG BANG CHICKEN

SALADE NIÇOISE

The french classic salad with a slight twist

SALAD FRENCH PREP COOKING 15m SALAD SPICY EASY

Description:
We've all had a salade niçoise. This one differs slightly in the addition of citrus notes in the olives and smoked anchovies.

Ingredients

- ◊ Tinned Tuna (HIGH QUALITY)
- ◊ New Potatoes
- ◊ Egg x 1
- ◊ Green beans
- ◊ Mixed baby tomatoes
- ◊ Smoked Anchovies
- ◊ Black Olives (in Orange)

or if unavailable marinated in orange peel)

- ◊ Olive Oil
- ◊ Lemon and Orange Zest

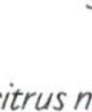

Vinaigrette

- ◊ Red Wine Vinegar
- ◊ Olive Oil
- ◊ Sea Salt
- ◊ Black Pepper

Tools

- ◊ Knife
- ◊ Glass Bowl
- ◊ Saucepans

Steps

Prep: Halve and boil new potatoes in salted water for 10-12 minutes. Blanch green beans for 5 minutes. Rinse both under cold water and let dry. Hard boil an egg for 12-14 minutes. (See BOILING AN EGG on page 73)

Assembly/Plating: Make a vinaigrette. (See MAKING A SALAD DRESSING on page 69) On the plate, arrange the ingredients in a pattern (the picture shows a cross, for instance). Slice egg in half as centrepiece. Drizzle dressing on top and season generously.

Une salade niçoise de ne pas oublier.

Notes

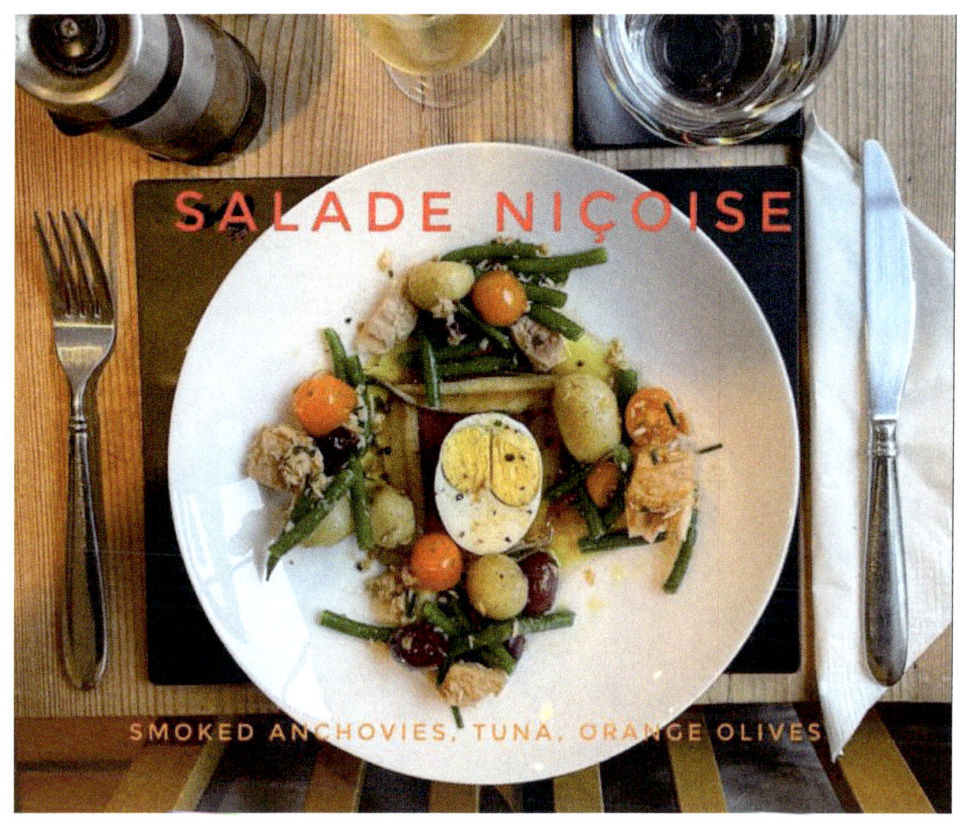
SALADE NIÇOISE
SMOKED ANCHOVIES, TUNA, ORANGE OLIVES

VITELLO TONNATO

Veal with Tuna Sauce

SALAD

ITALIAN

PREP COOKING

20m

SALAD

SPICY

EASY

Description:

Vitello Tonnato is an unspeakably rich and unique combination that makes you wonder what the original chef was thinking when he/she made it up, but it works magnificently, a perfect marriage between salty, sour, bitter, and creaminess.

Ingredients

- Veal Loin
- Tinned Tuna (HIGH QUALITY)
- Lime
- Egg yolks x 2
- Capers
- Anchovies
- Chives
- Celery
- Mixed baby tomatoes
- Lamb's Lettuce or Cress

Vinaigrette

- Red Wine Vinegar
- Olive Oil
- Sea Salt
- Black Pepper

Tools

- Knife
- Glass Bowl
- Frying Pan
- Spice Grinder or Blende

Steps

Prep: Roll veal loin in sea salt and pepper on board to coat evenly. Maillard Brown in frying pan for 2 minutes on all sides and leave to cool for 10 minutes. Make shaved Celery Ribbons with parer. In the spice grinder, blend one tin of tuna, juice of one lime, chopped chives, a teaspoon of capers, 4-5 anchovies, and two egg yolks. Drizzle in olive oil, and mix to a mayonnaise consistency. Season to taste (the capers and anchovies are strong, so go gently). Halve baby tomatoes. Make a vinaigrette. (See MAKING A SALAD DRESSING on page 69) Toss celery in the vinaigrette.

Assembly/Plating: Thinly slice the veal, top with the tonnato sauce and a few capers. Arrange all (tomatoes, veal, celery, and greens) in a row. Drizzle dressing on greens, then olive oil on top with a few grinds of pepper.

Pair with a chilled glass of white wine. Can also be a nice starter.

Notes

VITELLO TONNATO | SHAVED CELERY HEARTS

CHEF'S SALAD

Simple things done well are sometimes the best

SALAD

BRITISH

OVEN FOR PREP

NO COOKING

10m

SALAD

SPICY

EASY

Description:

The classic chef's salad depends on two things: the freshness and the quality of the ingredients and the tartness of the dressing. Thick ham, vintage cheddar, pop-in-the-mouth small tomatoes, a firm avocado, and crisp sourdough croutons. A sauce rose is the preferred dressing to add the tartness.

Ingredients

- ◊ Thickly sliced ham
- ◊ Vintage Cheddar
- ◊ Baby tomatoes (cherry, santini or teardrop)
- ◊ Avocado
- ◊ Romaine lettuce
- ◊ Sourdough croutons

Sauce Rose Dressing

- ◊ Mayonnaise (dollop)
- ◊ Greek Yoghurt (dollop)
- ◊ Red Wine Vinegar (capful)
- ◊ Ketchup
- ◊ Sea Salt and Black Pepper
- ◊ Olive Oil

Tools

- ◊ Knife
- ◊ Glass Bowl

Steps

Prep: Preheat oven to **175°C** (347°F). Cut one slice of sourdough bread into cubes for croutons.. Drizzle olive oil and season with sea salt from a height. Place on foil and put in oven for 7-10 minutes (keep an eye out they don't burn). Halve the tomatoes. Cut the ham, cheese, and avocado into uniform small cubes. Slice the lettuce horizontally and rinse and salad spin. Make the sauce rose. (See MAKING A CREAMY SALAD DRESSING on page 70)

Assembly/Plating: Thoroughly mix all ingredients in a bowl (save the croutons) and arrange on the plate with the lettuce as pictured. Top with the croutons. Have a bowl with the sauce to the side.

The kind of light supper that makes you feel refreshed, not too full, and good about yourself.

Notes

CHEF'S SALAD

CUCUMBER AND PALM HEARTS

A simple salad which is pretty and unique

SALAD | BRITISH | NO COOKING | 10m | SALAD | MILD | EASY

Description:
This salad is elegant in its simplicity. A cucumber is stuffed with a palm heart and has a vibrant pepper/tomato sauce.

Ingredients

- Cucumber x 1
- Tin of palm hearts
- Baby tomatoes x 2
- Lamb's lettuce

Tomato and Red Pepper Dressing

- Char-grilled Red Peppers in jar
- Baby tomatoes x 4
- Lime
- Sea Salt and Black Pepper
- Olive Oil

Tools

- Knife
- Glass Bowl
- Apple Corer
- Parer
- Spice Grinder

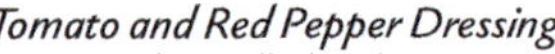

Steps

Prep: Peel and top and tail cucumber. Using an apple corer, remove the center of the cucumber with seeds. Replace with a palmito and slice horizontally to create the stuffed cucumber. For the sauce, combine baby tomatoes, red peppers, juice of ½ lime, olive oil, sea salt, and black pepper in the spice grinder and blitz until smooth. Season to taste.

Assembly/Plating: Put salad ingredients with lamb's lettuce and halved baby tomatoes in a small square bowl. Have the red pepper on the side in a ramekin for each individual portion, with a drizzle of olive oil as art.

A blink-or-you'll-hurt-your-eyes visual masterpiece. Very simple to make with the right tools.

Notes

CUCUMBER | PALMITOS
RED PEPPER TOMATO SAUCE

LARB GAI

Half-salad, half warm dish of spicy and umami goodness

SALAD | THAI | WOK | FAST COOKING | 30m | POULTRY | V. SPICY | EASY

Description:

A salad of minced chicken with crunchy roasted rice, galangal and lemon grass, red onion, and lime taught to me by Nog Suwankumpoo (R.I.P.), *matron chef of the Thai Elephant in Richmond in the early 2000s*

Ingredients

- ◊ Minced chicken (1 packet)
- ◊ Lime x 1
- ◊ Red Onion x 1
- ◊ Galangal (1 thumb-sized knob)
- ◊ Thai Sticky Rice (¼ cup)
- ◊ Bib lettuce
- ◊ Red Thai chillies x 2
- ◊ Palm or brown sugar (pinch)
- ◊ Lemon grass stalk x 1
- ◊ Garlic (1 clove)
- ◊ Thai Fish Sauce (Nam pla) (1 tblsp)
- ◊ Sriracha sauce (a few squirts)
- ◊ Chilli flakes
- ◊ Sea Salt and Black Pepper
- ◊ Olive Oil
- ◊ Kanom Jeep dumplings (store-bought)
- ◊ ***Dipping sauce*** Dark soy sauce (1 tblsp
- ◊ Rice Vinegar (1tblsp)
- ◊ Spring Onion x 1

Tools

- ◊ Frying pan
- ◊ Small copper pan for roasting rice
- ◊ Pestle & mortar
- ◊ Spice Grinder
- ◊ Glass bowl
- ◊ Chef's Knife
- ◊ Ramekins

Steps

Prep: Dice and crush galangal, garlic and lemon grass stalk in pestle & mortar and reserve paste. Roast rice in small copper pan until rice turns nutty and grind briefly in spice grinder (not too fine) with chilli flakes. Reserve. Slice red onion and red chilli. Make dipping sauce for *kanom jeep* with rice vinegar, dark soy, a pinch of sugar and finely chopped spring onions. ***Cooking:*** Heat wok to screaming hot. Pat dry chicken mince with paper towel and season with sea salt and pepper. Fry until starting to Maillard brown. Add sliced onion, chillies, and paste and stir fry for 2 minutes to take the bite out of the onion. Add lime juice, sugar, fish sauce, sriracha and olive oil and mix. Then add crushed rice for crunch. Steam or microwave kanom jeep dumplings which you can buy at an Asian store. ***Plating:*** Spoon *larb gai* on bib lettuce leaves and arrange dumplings. Put dipping sauce in a ramekin for easy dipping.

Eat the bib lettuce parcels with your hands. Keep some chopsticks for the kanom jeep.

Notes

LARB GAI | KANOM JEEP

ACKNOWLEDGEMENTS

This book has been a labour of love. But the love of food does not come from just anywhere. One is inspired by others, and by other people's dishes, or the quality of their produce. Then you aspire to be able to attempt some of the food you have tasted, and emulate some of the chefs who have led the way or do justice to the folks who have provided you with fine ingredients..

There is no knowing where this might come from. It is a shame that in my career many of the chefs I have encountered through meals all over the world have remained anonymous, only their food lodged in my memory.

Here are a few however of the people and the dishes who have inspired me the most.

Dominic Aslett, Head Chef at Blakeney House, Norfolk
Monica Gil Ruiz, chef patron of London Basque Kitchen
Manish Sharma, Head Chef at Delhi Social Club, Twickenham
Dai Ikeda, YouTube chef and patron of Bento-ya in London
Alex Payne, Executive Chef at The Tudor Pass
Jorge Toledo, Head Chef at Hotel Luca, Mexico City
Nog Suwankumpoo (RIP)- Head Chef at the Thai Elephant in Richmond (also RIP)

And artisans or purveyors of materials:

Steve & Aaron Young and Ben Murney of Pethers Butchers in Kew
Alex Mugan, Bray Cured Meats, in Bray (who taught me how to make chorizo)

And people on the web who have taught me (and countless others) a thing or two about the science of cooking

Blog.Thermoworks.com (the best source for info on heat and temperature)
Cooking for Geeks by Jeff Potter

And friends who have shepherded this manuscript through its production or helped and encouraged along the way:

Fuad and Sheila El Hadery, John Herbert, Diego Sanchez, Tet Ogino, and of course, my wife Christina, without whom none of this would have been conceived or even possible.

Dominic Aslett

Monica Gil Ruiz
LONDON
BASQUE
KITCHEN

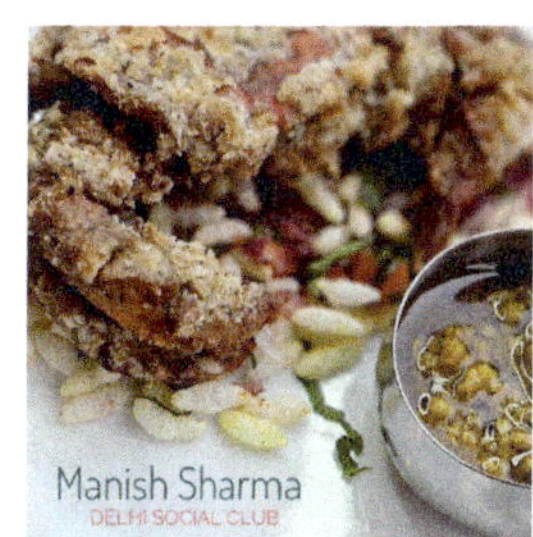
Manish Sharma
DELHI SOCIAL CLUB

Dai Ikeda
BENTO-YA

Four Dishes
by Alex Payne

Cizne
de Jorge Toledo

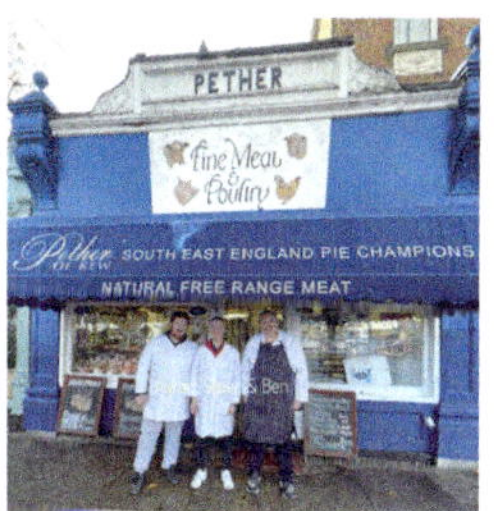
PETHER
Fine Meat & Poultry
Pether of Kew SOUTH EAST ENGLAND PIE CHAMPIONS
NATURAL FREE RANGE MEAT

Alex Mugan

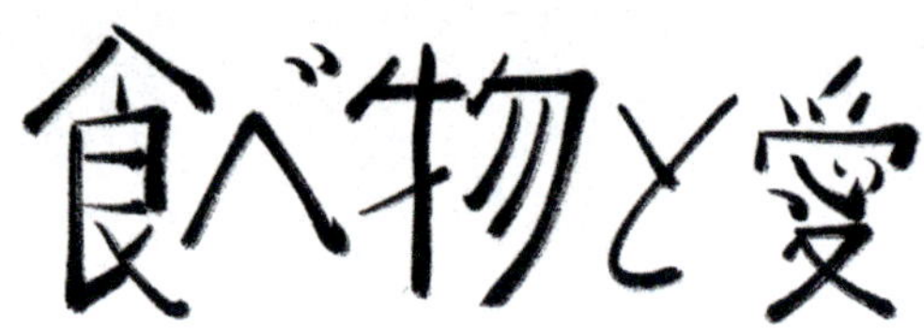

たべものとあい

FOOD AND LOVE

When you dream of food
You dream of love for both are
All about sharing.

INDEX

A

H

I

L

M

T

ABOUT THE AUTHOR

I was born in Caracas, Venezuela, raised in a small town in North Carolina named Tryon, and have lived all over the world, namely: Bogota and Barranquilla, Colombia, Tryon and Durham, North Carolina. Blandford Forum and London, England, Washington, New York, Boston, Paris, Geneva, Hong Kong, Seoul, and Tokyo. Since 1987 I have lived in London. Wherever I go, I am always dreaming of my next meal, and trying something I haven't had before.

I have been married to Christina for forty three years, and my son Roman, a doctor in the US, is a chef in his own right in addition to being a musician.

I am a graduate of Duke University and the Johns Hopkins School of Advanced International Studies. I am a photographer and author.

My name in kanji, given to me in Korea, is BECK DAE HO.

This means White Great Tiger, thus the provenance of the name of this book.

OTHER BOOKS BY D. ERIC PETTIGREW

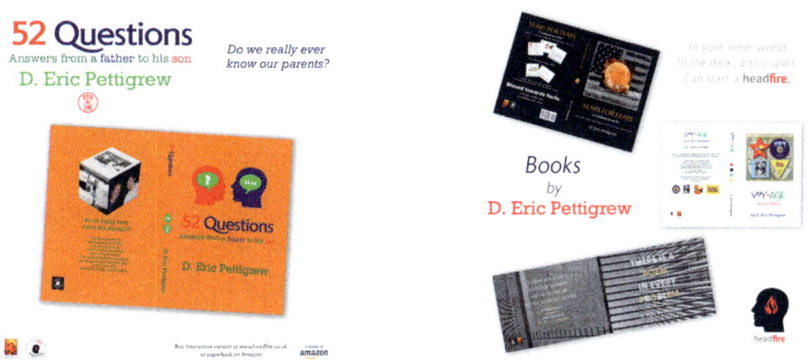

available at
amazon

Printed in Great Britain
by Amazon